THE TESTIMONY OF ST PAUL

Cover photograph:
Rome, St Paul's Basilica
Central door (detail)

Carlo M. Martini
Archbishop of Milan

THE TESTIMONY
OF ST PAUL

Meditations on the life and letters of St Paul

Translated by Susan Leslie

Crossroad • New York

1989

The Crossroad Publishing Company
370 Lexington Avenue, New York, N.Y. 10017

Original title: *Le Confessioni de Paolo*
Copyright © 1981 Editrice Ancora, Milan, Italy

English translation copyright © 1983 St. Paul Publications

Printed in the United States of America

Library of Congress Cataloging-in-Publication Data

Martini, Carlo M.
    [Confessioni di Paolo. English]
    The testimony of St. Paul : meditations on the life and letters of
St. Paul / Carlo M. Martini ; translated by Susan Leslie.
      p.   cm.
    Translation of: Le confessioni di Paolo.
    Reprint. Originally published: London, England : St. Paul
Publications, c1983.
    ISBN 0-8245-0958-7
    1. Paul, the Apostle, Saint—Meditations. 2. Bible. N.T.
Epistles of Paul—Meditations. I. Title. II. Title: Testimony of
Saint Paul.
BS2506.M38   1983
225.9'2—dc20   89-32867
                                              CIP

Contents

Foreword   7

1. On the road to Damascus   9
   False interpretations
   The mystery of Damascus
   Questions to ask ourselves

2. The knowledge of Jesus   17
   Where were you when the Word caught up with you?
   In which direction did the Lord take you?
   How did this transition come about?
   Let us ask ourselves a few questions, too

3. Paul's darkness   28
   Blindness as a reaction to the splendour of God
   Blindness as a way of penance
   Personal sin
   Root sin
   Structural sin

4. Conversion and disappointment   39
   The texts
   The actual facts
   The motivation behind the facts
   Paul's own experience
   A question to ask ourselves

5. Priestly examination of conscience   50
   "To be with"
   "I have served the Lord"
   "With tears"
   "In all humility"

6. Conversion and estrangement   61
   Who was Barnabas?
   What Barnabas was to Paul
   What happened?
   What were the consequences?
   How Paul experienced the separation

7. The transfiguration of Paul   73
   What is meant by transfiguration
   Inner attitudes of transfiguration
   The outward manifestations of Paul's transfiguration
   Paul's transfiguration is the model for the
       transfiguration of the pastor

8. Passio Pauli, passio Christi   84
   Similarities and differences between 'passio Christi'
       and 'passio Pauli'
   The passion of the Christian
   How Paul particularly shared in the passion of Christ
   Questions for us

9. God is mercy   95
   Paul's last words
   Conclusion

Foreword

Paul is a most enigmatic saint. Certainly his most loved and best known passage is the glorious hymn to love in 1 Corinthians chapter 13. Yet he is also popularly reputed as a mysogynist (he was not, in fact, but he shared with his contemporaries the feeling that women should be kept in their place . . .). His prolific pen was capable of warm encouragement and praise as well as stern rebuke. His theology is expressed in majestic poetry and in complicated and repetitive prose. Peter the fisherman is not the only one to have found that "our beloved brother Paul . . . has written . . . some things hard to be understood" (2 Peter 3 : 15-16).

All in all, it is difficult for most of us to form a coherent picture of this many-faceted Apostle. Fortunately, Archbishop Martini comes to our aid with this absorbing and helpful study of St Paul.

Carlo Maria Martini imagines Paul on his way to his execution. It is said that the last moments before death are often preceded by a review of one's entire life. If we had stopped to speak to Paul as he faced martyrdom, what would he have told us? What would have been the most significant moments of his life? What would have been his final testimony?

Archbishop Martini starts with what he considers to be the touchstone of Paul's vocation and ministry: the vision of Christ on the road to Damascus. Deftly, he separates the profound from the more superficial aspects of Paul's 'conversion' — and goes on to ask us some searching questions about our own conversion.

The rest of the book follows the same pattern of: an episode from Paul's life; an extended commentary, drawing on his letters; and a series of questions for us to answer about our own journey to God.

Archbishop Martini is a fine biblical scholar and he is also an excellent teacher. This enables him to lead us with authority and clarity in a consideration of Paul's thoughts and attitudes. Above all, he helps us to understand and to reconcile: Paul the fiery orator, Paul the tender and devoted servant of Christ, Paul the teacher and pastor, Paul the impetuous soul who humbly admits his weakness and expects all from the merciful grace of God.

These meditations were originally retreat addresses given to priests in the diocese of Milan. As such they naturally place a certain emphasis on pastoral activities and duties. However there is nothing 'technical' or exclusive here: the Archbishop's wise and penetrating comments are for all of us. He discusses the knowledge of Jesus, conversion and disappointment, the transformation of the Christian by God's grace. These are topics which are vital for every Christian.

There is also a sensitive analysis of Paul's quarrel with Barnabas and its lesson for us in our relationships with our own colleagues. In a helpful chapter on sin and penitence, Archbishop Martini distinguishes between 'personal', 'root' and 'structural' sin. We are also led to consider the passion of Christ and of his saints with reference to our own sufferings and trials. In the final chapter — a detailed study of parts of Paul's farewell address at Miletus — the Archbishop presents a synthesis of Paul's message and stresses that he is above all the Apostle of grace.

This is a book to be read slowly and prayerfully. It would also be ideal for Bible study groups as it includes such thought-provoking questions as well as such beautiful opening prayers.

Paul was a key figure in the early Church and has influenced every age of Christianity up to our own. Archbishop Martini repeatedly insists that we can understand but little of the Apostle's fascinating and many-sided personality. But this little he shares with us in a series of wise and sometimes moving meditations which evidently spring from profound study and deep reverence for the saint. What seems to be 'little' to Archbishop Martini seems to us to be 'much'.

S.L.

On the road to Damascus

In these meditations on the testimony of St Paul, the chapters are written in pairs; in the first of each pair we shall look at an episode relating to Paul's conversion, trying to enter into it imaginatively; in the second, we shall study the doctrinal and spiritual themes of the first chapter in the light of Paul's letters.

The first conversion episode takes place on the road to Damascus. In fact if we had asked Paul, as he prepared for martyrdom, what had been the decisive moment of his life, he would undoubtedly have replied: the vision on the road to Damascus.

The whole life of the Apostle was marked by that event. It is difficult for us to understand it for in fact, it was only at the point of death that Paul himself understood its full meaning. We ourselves will probably have to wait until the end of our life's journey before we fully grasp the meaning of our baptism or ordination.

On the other hand, even if it is difficult to take Damascus as our starting-point — because it is the episode which includes everything else and which can only be understood in the light of successive conversion experiences — it is nevertheless quite certain that, as far as Paul is concerned, everything starts from there.

Before everything was different; *afterwards* everything will be different.

False interpretations

1. Let us start by getting rid of any false ideas we may have about this event.

It is a story so often repeated in catechesis, liturgy and art as to have become somewhat hackneyed — think of all those familiar illustrations which feature the horse, Paul falling to the ground, the bright light. It is all too easy to misunderstand, trivialize and underrate the whole episode,

9

with serious consequences for our understanding of God's dealings with man.

— One false, or at least incomplete, idea is to look at Damascus purely as a moral conversion: Paul was a great sinner and, at a certain point, having understood what harm he was doing, he changed his way of life. This is conversion seen on an ethical level denoting Paul's strong will, his profound change of heart and movement towards an interior life.

From this viewpoint, all the emphasis is on what Paul was, what makes him change, what he becomes.

— Another narrow interpretation is to think of Paul as *a man who transfers his allegiance*. A zealous observer of the Law who, from a certain point onwards, dedicates his zeal, oratorical skill and tireless activity to the service of a new master, Christ.

This is nothing more than a change of objective, a change of Church: first he served the Synagogue, then the Church of Christ whom he came to see as the triumphant Way. In the Christian life, too, we call 'conversion' what is in fact a transfer of allegiance; sometimes the people concerned even transfer their allegiance to a third master.

Or we may think that the whole thing was caused by the force of his own energies which were originally concentrated on one thing and then transferred to something which seemed better. At that rate, he may even end up by returning to the first thing so creating confusion among those who no longer understood what is happening.

It is not a question of a conversion but simply of changing camps.

If we interpret Paul's conversion like this, we shall very likely apply such norms to our own or others' conversion and so greatly underestimate the action of God.

2. Instead, let us try to get rid of all the words we have put into Paul's mouth or that we thought he had said about his conversion.

The first thing we must throw out is the word 'conversion' itself.

I wonder if it is accurate to speak of 'Paul's conversion',

since he never used that term for the event of Damascus. Perhaps we have understood very little of what actually happened to him; we have classified it in a certain way, reducing it to a category which is simple but far from exhaustive.

We know that the term 'conversion' is typical of the New Testament: today, in our own tradition, we read 'conversion' where more ancient traditions, influenced above all by the Vulgate, spoke of 'repentance'. There has evidently been a change of language.

At one time, Jesus' first words, recorded in Mark 1:15, were translated: "Repent and believe the Gospel". This was from the Latin *paenitemini*.

Nowadays we translate it "be converted". The word 'conversion' has taken the place of 'repent' or 'do penance'.

In the New Testament there is a specific vocabulary dealing with conversion, which it is well to remember because it helps us to understand translations which are far from exact.

The term 'conversion' is typical of the Bible which uses the Hebrew word 'sub' meaning 'to return'.

Strictly speaking, conversion is a movement in which one goes in one direction and at a certain point, stops and goes back in the opposite direction.

In the New Testament the idea of returning is expressed mainly by two verbs which we find in the Synoptics and in Acts: 'metanoein' which means a change of mind, and 'epistrefo' which actually means 'to return'.

In Mark 1:15: "The time is fulfilled, the Kingdom of God is near, be converted and believe the Gospel", the word is 'metanoeite'. In Acts 3:19 (Peter's second speech) we find both 'metanoein' and 'epistrefo': "Repent, then, and change your way of life, for your sins are forgiven". 'Repent' is used here for variety — the other expression already has the word 'change' in it — but the sense is the same: a change of mind or return.

The word 'repent' also has a precise meaning; it refers either to the inner sorrow at what one has done or to the forms of penance which one undertakes in token of future amendment. All these words have the basic meaning of 'returning'. According to Acts, Paul himself uses this language when he sums up his preaching: "I urged the pagans to *be converted* and to *return* to God, doing the works of true repentance" (Acts 26:20); the two verbs are 'metanoein' and 'epistrefein'; and he also speaks of works of 'metanoias'.

This makes it all the more surprising that the Apostle should never have described his own experience with the word 'conversion'. He does not mention having done anything which can be defined as 'metanoein' or 'epistrefein'.

Paul knew very well what a conversion was and he knew that his own had all the characteristics of a conversion. However, his experience took a greater and more profound form. It should also be noted that while the Synoptics and Acts use 'conversion' vocabulary frequently, John never does so. This shows that in the New Testament there are different ways of viewing the complex phenomenon of man's journey to God. John prefers to say: to come to Jesus, to come to him, to walk towards him. The basic concept of conversion — which is thoroughly biblical — is expressed in the fourth Gospel in terms of following Jesus and personal relationship with him. This is nearer to Paul's interpretation of his own conversion.

The mystery of Damascus

Having cleared away these false and inadequate interpretations, let us see how the Apostle describes the event of Damascus.

The first surprising fact is that he refers to it so seldom. He is almost completely silent about the fundamental experience whose implications he develops in all his letters. At the time of his death, I imagine that it is the one episode which stood clearly before his eyes; yet in all his highly autobiographical writings he hardly ever mentions it directly. Perhaps it was more important for Paul to integrate Damascus into his life and theology, to live and to apply the experience rather than to talk about it.

12

Which are the few texts that mention it?

a) In the longer letters, the only basic text in which the Damascus vision is described is Galatians: "But when he who chose me even from my mother's womb and called me by his grace, was pleased to reveal his Son to me so that I might proclaim him among the Gentiles . . ." (Galatians 1:15-16). Paul uses four verbs: he *chose* me . . . he *called* me . . . he was pleased to *reveal* . . . so that I might *proclaim* him. Only the third verb refers directly to conversion. The others place conversion within the framework of divine providence: he chose me, he was pleased, that is, he decided, he wished to reveal himself to me.

So the experience is described essentially as the revelation of the Son to him (according to the Greek text 'in' him) and for the sake of a mission.

b) In a passage in the letter to the Romans, Paul transfers his own experience to a general setting: "For those whom he has known from eternity he has also predestined to be conformed to the image of his Son, so that he might be the first-born of many brothers; those whom he predestined he also called; those whom he called he also justified; those whom he justified he also glorified" (Romans 8:29-30).

c) In the first letter to the Corinthians there is a very brief allusion, in a polemical context: "Am I not free? Am I not an apostle? Have I not seen the Lord Jesus?" (1 Corinthians 9:1): Damascus was a 'seeing' of the Lord. And further on in the same letter: "After all the others he appeared to me also, as to one born at the wrong time. I am in fact the least of the apostles, and am not even worthy to be called an apostle because I persecuted the Church of God" (1 Corinthians 15:8-9). The man who persecuted the Church describes the event of Damascus as an apparition "to me, unworthy as I was". There are indeed elements of moral conversion; but the simple fact is: Jesus appeared.

d) There is another passage which is important because, although it does not actually speak of the event, it describes how Paul experienced it: "If anyone thinks he has reason to trust in the flesh, I have still more: circumcised on the eighth day, of the stock of Israel and the tribe of Benjamin, a Hebrew born of Hebrews, in legal observance, a Pharisee; as for zeal, I was a persecutor of the Church; as for the righteousness which comes from keeping the Law, I was beyond reproach. But what could be a gain to me I have come to consider as a loss because of Christ. Rather, from now on, I consider everything as loss compared with the knowledge of Christ Jesus my Lord, for whom I have suffered the loss of all these things which I consider as so much rubbish so that I may win Christ and be found in him, not with my own righteousness derived from the Law but with that which comes from faith in Christ, that is, the righteousness which comes from God and is based on faith" (Philippians 3:4-9).

Paul's first and last states are described in terms of possession and poverty (involving a new possession of Christ). But the description of all the things he formerly possessed, should make us think. In the letter to the Corinthians he wrote: "I am the least of all" (we would say 'a sinner'); now he says of himself: "with regard to keeping the Law, I was beyond reproach". That is why it is not easy to use the categories of 'sinner' and 'blasphemer' when speaking of Paul.

If he is 'beyond reproach', what has changed? "What could be a gain to me I have come to consider as a loss because of Christ". His whole world has undergone a revolutionary change; what he formerly thought important now seems negligible to him and holds no importance at all. The things which he would never have renounced before, he now considers as so much rubbish because the knowledge of Christ has assumed absolute primacy for him and fills every aspect of his life. The encounter, knowledge and fullness of Christ have completely altered his previous judgments and values.

e) Another important text: "God, who said: Let the light shine in the darkness, has shone in our hearts that we might be enlightened by the knowledge of the divine glory shining in the face of Christ" (2 Corinthians 4:6). Here the

14

reference is to every apostle, but it is particularly appropriate in the case of Paul's conversion. The God of creation shines in his heart and illuminates it to make him understand the riches of Christ, his life.

f) The last passage gives us the best clue to Paul's moral conversion. It would not be right to omit it, although it presents certain linguistic difficulties. "I give thanks to him who has given me strength, Christ Jesus Our Lord, for he has judged me trustworthy by calling me to the ministry: I who at first was a blasphemer, a violent man and a persecutor" (1 Timothy 1:12-13).

Was he then a blasphemer and a violent man? Was he in fact beyond reproach — as he writes to the Philippians — or was he a sinner from the point of view of morals?

He goes on: "But he showed mercy on me, because I acted without knowing him, far from the true faith; thus the grace of God was given to me in abundance along with the faith and the charity which is in Christ Jesus. This saying is true and worthy of universal acceptance: Christ Jesus came into the world to save sinners and I am the first among them. But precisely because of this I have been shown mercy for Jesus Christ to show his generosity first of all in my case, by way of example to all those who were to believe in him and so win eternal life" (1 Timothy 1:13-16).

Here we have the whole incomprehensible and profound mystery of this conversion.

So the Damascus event is much more complex than a simple case of moral conversion or change of mind. It is something so profound that we should approach it with great humility and reverence, realizing that we know and understand very little about it, but by the grace of God we can learn much moie. As a result, we shall gain a deeper understanding of ourselves, our own journey through life and our own conversion.

Questions to ask ourselves

Let us end by asking ourselves a basic question in keeping with this meditation: when was I converted? Is there a

15

specific moment of conversion in my life to which I can refer as to an historic event? Even if there is not such a specific moment, there have certainly been moments of change, of turning round, of crisis which have brought us a fresh understanding of the mystery of God.

If we have never really experienced this fundamental change of mind which is essential to the Christian life, we have not yet grasped the meaning of the essential newness of the Christian way, which involves turning round and going in the opposite direction.

If you do not really understand what has been said about Paul, you probably do not fully understand what has happened to you. In that case, we need to turn to prayer, saying:

> Lord, help me to know my way. Help me, as Jeremiah says, to set up signposts in my past: "Review the ways of the past and set up signposts". Help me to understand the various stages of your plan for my life, the moments of light and darkness, the trials, when my endurance was stretched to the limit. Help me to know what stage I have reached on this way and where I stand. I ask this through Christ our Lord. Amen.

The knowledge of Jesus

Let us now try to deepen our understanding of the Damascus episode as Paul seeks to do in some of his letters. Let us admit our diffidence when seeking to penetrate the mystery of God in another soul, even though Paul is a symbolic figure for all Christendom.

Let us also freely admit our inability to grasp the full meaning of the texts. May the Lord have mercy on us and help us to glimpse something of that indescribable light which surrounded and transformed the life of the Apostle.

We turn directly to you, Apostle Paul. You see how presumptuously we are attempting to penetrate the mystery of your life over which you yourself pondered for so many years. If we do so, it is because we desire to know you by the knowledge of what God has done in you; we want to know who God is, who Jesus Christ is, who Jesus is for us. We know that you, Paul, far from being indifferent, actually share this desire of ours. It is for this that you lived and suffered and died. It is because of your suffering and death that we pray to you now. Open our eyes as the Lord opened yours, so that we may understand the power of God in you and the power of God in us. Help us to know what you were before your conversion and what we were before God called us and how we stand now, as we face God's call.

We turn to you, too, Apostle Matthew, so that, proceeding from what we think we know and have already understood, we may enter the boundless territory of the Word of God.

In this boundless territory may we find the nourishment, the water and manna which will enable us to travel, the fire which will warm and illuminate us; let us listen to the Word of God, let us see the lightning flash of his glory.

May we, like Paul and Matthew, proclaim your message courageously in freedom of speech and spirit.

Hear, O Father, the prayer which we make to you with the Apostles Paul and Matthew and also with Mary Mother of Jesus. Through Christ our Lord. Amen.

In order to understand the wealth of the divine action in Paul, to understand what he himself said of his experience (an experience which millions take as their point of reference), it is useful to add to the already quoted texts the three descriptions of his conversion which may be found in Acts chapter 9 — in the third person — and in chapters 22 and 26 in autobiographical form.

The description in chapter 26 is the richest in autobiographical detail and is also the longest and most extensive. This can serve as our starting-point; it will help us to clarify the questions we need to ask Paul and we can listen to the answers he gives us both in Acts and in the letters already mentioned. It is the last speech Paul made in his defence before Agrippa at Caesarea.

Recently the remains of the imperial palace have been discovered: and it was there, by the sea, where the waves now break over the ruins of the Roman buildings, that Paul said of himself: "At one time, I, too, believed it my duty [he had a strong sense of duty] to take action against the name of Jesus of Nazareth as indeed I did at Jerusalem; I had many of the faithful imprisoned with the authorization of the high priests and when they were condemned to death, I also voted against them [he is obviously referring to the case of Stephen whose death he approved even though he did not actually throw the stones]. In all the synagogues I tried by torture to make them blaspheme and being absolutely furious with them I pursued them as far as foreign cities" (Acts 26:9-11).

There is a problem of historical criticism here. It does not appear that the Sanhedrin, at that time, had any authority outside the synagogues of Palestine and in the synagogues themselves its power was limited and certainly did not extend to the death penalty. The very killing of Stephen was probably a spontaneous act, the result of a popular uprising and certainly illegal. The synagogues had the power to interrogate, flog and impose certain punishments and it is in this sphere that Paul originally operated. Historians are therefore dubious about the reference to 'foreign cities'. Perhaps Paul obtained letters of recommendation and then, more zealous than the rest, he went off to these cities to win them over and to persecute the Christians. He was a man of great initiative when it was a question of what he considered just persecution: "Things being like this, while I was on the way to Damascus armed with authorizations and full powers from the high priests, towards midday I saw on the road, O King, a light from heaven brighter than the sun, which shone round me and my companions" (Acts 26: 12-13).

These words should be studied carefully: "a light from heaven". Paul pondered much on this and he will return to it when writing to the Corinthians: "The God, who said: Let there be light, is the one who has shone in our hearts" (2 Corinthians 4: 6).

The God of creation, who created every light, has manifested himself to him with an even greater light: Paul links all the great creative acts of God in the Old Testament with what has happened to him. The dazzling light which rose before his eyes was the glory of Christ himself beside which all other lights grow dim.

"We all fell to the ground and I heard a voice from heaven saying to me in Hebrew: Saul, Saul, why are you persecuting me? It is hard for you to kick against the goad. And I said: Who are you, Lord? And the Lord replied: I am Jesus whom you are persecuting. Get up and stand on your feet: I have appeared to you in order to make you a minister and witness both of those things you have seen and those which I will show you later. So I will save you from the people and from the Gentiles to whom I send you. You are to open their eyes so that they may pass from darkness to light and from the power of Satan to God, so that their sins may be forgiven and they may share the

inheritance of those who are sanctified by faith in me"
(Acts 26:14-18).

Putting this text alongside the others, we can ask Paul
these questions:

— What was the situation out of which the Lord
called you on the Damascus road and where were you
when the Word of God caught up with you?

— In which direction did this fundamental event in
your life take you?

— How did it come about, this passover of yours from
death to life, from darkness to light, from not knowing
God to knowing him?

Here are some possible answers.

Where were you when the Word caught up with you?

The answer is in the autobiographical passage in the
letter to the Philippians, where Paul affirms that the Word
of God reached him when he was in full possession of
certain fundamental values, dear to him and won, in part,
at great personal cost: "Although I, too, could have confidence in the flesh" (Philippians 3:4). These are the good
things which come to man from his own nature and history,
the work of his own hands: "I have all the more reason to
boast". These are the things that belong to the glorious
history of Paul:

— *circumcised on the eighth day*: not like the pagans
who were contemptuously termed 'the uncircumcised', in
the sense of accursed, abandoned, with whom God does not
seem to be concerned;

— *of the stock of Israel*: of the Chosen People, the
light of the nations;

— *of the tribe of Benjamin*: I am aware of my own
past, the ties of blood which go right back to the son of
Jacob:

— *a Hebrew born of Hebrews*: I possess a rich heritage, that is, my father and mother and grandparents are
all of that same glorious race;

— *in matters of legal observance, a Pharisee*: that is,
a Hebrew of the strict observance, keeping to an absolutely

20

rigorous moral code, the most versed in the Law, holding in tension the most profound elements of Jewish spirituality. Pharisee was the proud name which denoted a life of zealous legal observance requiring great inner moral application. _{NB}

— *As for zeal, I was a persecutor of the Church; as for the righteousness which comes from keeping the Law, I was beyond reproach.* This is the same praise which was given to Joseph: a righteous man. John the Baptist's parents, and Joachim and Anna are also described like this: they were righteous. Paul was in fact describing himself from the biblical point of view, in terms of the highest praise.

— *Beyond reproach*: He could have said: "Which of you could convict me of sin?"

— *As for my keeping of the Law, no one could have found fault with that*: we know how detailed were the commandments and ceremonial prescriptions and how complicated the rituals. Even today Jewish food laws are various and complicated; certain foods are prescribed, others may not be taken at all, others have to be checked for origin. All in all, this requires considerable spiritual application. Paul, then, is taken in a situation in which he possesses traditions, personal commitment, zeal, righteousness: all these things are extremely valuable to him and he enumerates them with deep emotion.

One needs to have known Jewish people in order to realize how intensely proud they are, even today, of their race and tradition, their very Jewishness. It is something that is second nature to them, a way of life which they cannot renounce. Simone Weil is a typical example. She had a very deep understanding of the mysteries of Baptism and the Eucharist and of prayer; she wrote some of the most beautiful pages ever written on the Christian life, on work and contemplation; but she was never baptized herself because she felt she could not renounce her Jewishness. In spite of a profound appreciation of the beauty of Christian truth and a longing to feed on the Eucharist, in which she saw the culmination of history and creation, she was hindered to the last by what she considered to be her traditional heritage and by the need of solidarity with her own martyred people.

In the letter to the Philippians, Paul always uses an expression which refers to Jesus but which, seen in this light, certainly has an autobiographical flavour: "Jesus Christ, though by nature divine, did not consider his equality with God as a treasure to be jealously guarded". The Greek words seem to mean: "he did not consider it as *booty*", that is, something to be grasped and held onto greedily. This is how Paul thought of his religious heritage: a *treasure* to be jealously guarded and relinquished to no one. As a result he took great care to guard this treasure of his, to foster it and to defend it violently against all attacks.

This explains his intolerance towards the Christians and the need to exterminate them, because he realized, quite rightly, that they were undermining the very foundations of his 'treasure'.

We are now in a position to understand Paul's self-accusations, to which the first letter to Timothy refers: "I had been a blasphemer, a persecutor, a violent man" (1 Timothy 1:13). Not a blasphemer in the sense that he turned against God but in the sense that, without knowing it — and that is the meaning of his conversion and the central drama of his life — he turned against Christ the Son of God, in order to defend his treasure. Now we can see why he described his life as sinful for, in fact — and he will realize it more and more clearly — his attitude to God was a profoundly mistaken one. He did not look on God as God, author and origin of all good; his life was centred on *his* possessions, *his* truth, the treasures which had been entrusted to *him*, Paul. Outwardly, his attitude was indeed 'beyond reproach', but inwardly it was merely an extreme possessiveness which cut at the very roots of his relationship with the God who is both Father and Creator.

This was the basic confusion in which he lived without knowing it and from which will spring his new under-

22

standing of the Gospel, of grace and mercy, the divine initiative and the activity of God.

He was living, not by the Gospel of grace but by the law of self-justification which made him forget that he was a poor man pardoned by God not because he was something in himself but because God loved him.

The drama of Paul's life is subtle and difficult — it is the drama of a profundly religious man which nearly led to a radical distortion of God's image in him.

This is the situation which Paul came from, a situation of ideological violence.

Ideological violence, the fruit of fanaticism or the inability to understand others unless they are submissive to one's own ideas, has not disappeared in our times. Man is still seeking his own salvation, his own righteousness and self-justification which leads to every sort of aberration; this comes of being set in the belief that one is an absolute master rather than a servant of truth.

Paul's situation can throw light on some of the worst perversions. Jesus attacked these perversions in the Gospel when he said: "The sinners will go into the Kingdom of God before you". He means that the man who commits sins, of drunkenness or sensuality for example, is certainly a sinner but is always in some way aware of his wrong doing: he needs understanding, help and compassion in order to overcome his own weakness and he admits his frailty. This is the sin which Jesus attacks in the Pharisees: the basic perversion by which man sets himself up as his own salvation, thinking himself on the heights of perfection and falling into the most serious aberrations of violence.

In which direction did the Lord take you?

Paul himself explains the significance of this direction in the letters to the Philippians and Galatians.

a) First of all the Lord led him towards a total detachment from what had seemed supremely important to him before: "What would have been gain to me, I have considered loss because of Christ. Rather, from now on I consider everything as loss compared with the knowledge of Jesus Christ my Lord for whom I have suffered the loss of all these things which I count as so much rubbish, so that I may win Christ" (Philippians 3 : 7-8).

The Lord led him to realize that all this is worthless compared with Christ: not in itself, but compared with Christ.

He was led to a completely new outlook on everything. This was not an instant moral change but rather a moment of illumination: he speaks of revelations because, as he looks at things from a new standpoint, that of Christ, everything seems different to him. Now he judges his life so very differently that the exclamation which best sums up his inner response to Jesus' words on the Damascus road is this: I have got everything wrong! What I thought was of value was *not* and I have allowed myself to be drawn into acts which are violent and in fact unjust. I who glorified in my own righteousness have become an executioner of the innocent.

As Jesus asks him, "Why are you persecuting me?" he understands, in a flash, that he has miserably failed to see the truth. One can see what a terrible shock it must have been to Paul: it is not by reasoning but by an immediate contact with the truth that he comes to understand that he must start all over again and turn his whole life upside down.

Similarly, Matthew chapter 13 describes a merchant who, having found one precious pearl, realizes that all the rest are worthless; and there is the man who, having found a treasure hidden in a field, understands that everything else is meaningless.

Paul was confronted with such a revelation of Being that it made him change his ideas and attitude about what he was and what he was doing: it was a revelation which reversed his whole inner attitude.

b) A second indication of what direction he was taking can be found above all in the letter to the Galatians: "He was pleased to reveal his Son to me so that I might preach him among the Gentiles" (Galatians 1:15). This is the *mission* entrusted to Paul. It is disturbing for Paul that these two things should come together: at the same moment when Jesus makes him realize "I have got everything wrong", he says to him: "I entrust everything to you", I am sending you.

The compassionate God of the Gospel is he who, in the very moment when he shows me that I have totally misunderstood him, because I have put myself in his place, shows me his mercy by forgiving me and demonstrates his trust by calling me to his service, entrusting me with his very Word.

This moment sums up for Paul all the mistaken ideas he had of God. Darkness becomes light and violence is changed into mercy.

How did this transition come about?

We need to know what was revealed to Paul and why he speaks of *revelation* rather than conversion.

— *Everything was given to him as a gift:* it was not the outcome of his own efforts, meditations, spiritual exercises, long prayers and fasts. Everything was given to him, so that he would be a *sign* to all people of the mercy of God whose initiative always precedes our search for him.

It is a good idea to take a closer look at verse 15 of chapter 1 of the letter to the Galatians which uses Old Testament language to describe what happened to Paul: "When he who chose me from my mother's womb and called me by his grace was pleased to reveal his Son to me . . . ". The subject of the conversion is not Paul: it is God. The whole burden is on God's side, he is the author of the conversion.

As in the creation "God spoke and it was made", so in conversion, the initiative is his, quite apart from any merit, desire or thought of ours. God calls us and is pleased to manifest his Son to us.

This is the first aspect of 'how': through grace, as a gift, because it pleases God.

— *All his knowledge of Christ was given to him.* We have already seen that Paul, in fact, describes his conversion in terms of a meeting (1 Corinthians 15:8). Christ is the revelation of the divine initiative and mercy shown to me. Christ is where Paul meets God.

Let us ask ourselves a few questions, too

— In what way does my own experience resemble or differ from Paul's? In what way is it analogous? How can I perceive God's prevenient action in my life, which has made me what I am?

— Jesus was for Paul the manifestation of the divine mercy — how and in what way is he the basic point of reference for me, enabling me to understand who and what I am, where I have come from and what I am called to?

— What are the possessions which prevent me from making a free response to the divine initiative in my life?

We need to ask ourselves these questions in a spirit of love: if we do so in a spirit of possessiveness or self-justification, we will give hurried answers and will not be able to look deeply at the story of our life in God's sight. But if we ask in a spirit of love and mercy we shall see clearly what is the work of God in us and in what ways, like Paul, we are resisting his will.

Let us end by re-reading the account in 1 Timothy 1:15ff: "This word is reliable and worthy of full acceptance: Christ Jesus came into the world to save sinners of whom I am the chief".

Man's basic sin, which is at the root of all sins, is not to acknowledge God as God, the failure to see oneself as his gift, the fruit of his love: this is the satanic attitude of man's opposition to God. Paul had this attitude: thinking that he himself possessed so many good things, he was in fact refusing to receive God's goodness.

We are all capable of failing to recognize God as God. "And of these I am the chief. But precisely because of this, I have had mercy shown me, for Jesus Christ wanted to show through me, first of all, his great mercy as an example to all those who should believe in him and so gain eternal life".

This is why we are making these meditations about Paul who was a sign for others, for history and for the world.

"To the one immortal, invisible God of the ages, be honour and glory for ever and ever".

May the one God, who alone is worthy of honour and glory for what he has done and is doing in us, grant us to live with these words of praise in our hearts.

Paul's darkness

Let us take a closer look at one aspect of the event of Damascus: the "blindness" which follows immediately on Paul's conversion. Not only the darkness of the historical Paul but of the Paul who represents man in such a time of darkness.

This is a difficult subject because it touches on our own inner darkness which we never like to face. It is a penitential theme. Let us ask for the grace of the Holy Spirit that we may proceed in truth and openness of heart:

O Lord, you who search us out and know us, you know how incapable we are of understanding your mystery and our own. You know how unable we are to talk of these things truthfully. We ask you, Father, in the name of Jesus: send your Spirit who searches out the depths of man, who knows what is in us, that he may help us to know ourselves as we are known by you with love and mercy even in the depths of our sinfulness. Help us to see clearly the things that weigh us down, the ways in which we are rebellious or impervious to your grace; help us to look at these things in the merciful light which comes from the death and resurrection of your Son, Jesus Christ our Lord, who with the Spirit lives and reigns throughout the ages. Amen.

It was important to define Paul's conversion as 'revelation and enlightenment'. Now we need to ask how it happened that after his conversion Paul was blind.

This fact is stressed, somewhat emphatically, in the account of Acts: "Saul rose from the ground but when he opened his eyes he could see nothing. So, leading him by the hand, they took him to Damascus where he remained for three days without sight, neither eating nor drinking" (Acts 9: 8-9). One would almost think that the enlightenment of Christ, instead of filling him with joy, light and clarity, had struck him down as if with a serious illness; he cannot see or feed himself and he has to be led by the hand.

Later on the same thing is repeated: "And as I could no longer see, because of the brilliance of that light, I came to Damascus, my companions leading me by the hand" (Acts 22:11). He received his sight back when Ananias came and said to him: "Brother Saul, receive your sight! And at that moment I looked at him and I could see again" (Acts 22:13).

Why was Paul struck with blindness after the mysterious light of Christ was revealed to him?

Blindness in Scripture is clearly linked with sin and the disorientation of a man who staggers without any sense of direction. It is a punishment. Elymas in Cyprus was struck blind as a punishment: "Saul, also called Paul, filled with the Holy Spirit, fixed his eyes on him and said: O man full of deceit and every kind of malice, son of the devil, enemy of all that is good, when will you stop perverting the true ways of God? See, the Lord's hand is on you: you will be blind and for a time you will not see the sun" (Acts 13:9-11). In Elymas' case, however, the symbolic meaning of blindness is very clearly explained: he must stop perverting the true ways of God, behaving in a way that distorts the true image of God. Thus he is the symbol of man unable to find the right path, man imprisoned by the powers of Satan, "son of the devil"; and the result is that he is "enemy of all good".

Paul's blindness, on the other hand, is difficult to understand because the Acts of the Apostles does not explain it but confines itself to describing the fact, to which the Apostle never seems to allude in his letters.

As we reflect on this, trying to enter into his mind, two reasons emerge.

Blindness as a reaction to the splendour of God

First of all there is a recurrent biblical theme: "Man cannot see God and live". The vision of God is light but to man's carnal nature this is a fearful thing and it reveals to man all his own darkness. In contact with the God who is light, man realizes that he is darkness. Thus Paul does the sort of penance which he had never been able to do before. The knowledge of the glory of Christ is reflected in the knowledge of his own darkness and Paul experiences the true symbol of this until the word of Ananias, which is the word of the Church, intervenes, giving him a sense of acceptance into the Church and the assurance that he is walking in the way of God.

Blindness is the negative reaction to the glory of God which has been manifested to him. It is typical of Christian conversion that a man should gain much more self-knowledge and be more afraid of his own darkness when he becomes aware of God's light than when he subjects himself to self-examination or a sort of psychoanalysis of his own depths. It is the contact with the face of Christ which reveals to man his own darkness!

Blindness as a way of penance

The second reason for Paul's blindness is his sharing in the sin of the world, his partaking of sinful humanity.

Let us see how he experienced this and how it appeared to him.

There is no need for us to rely on our imagination because on several occasions Paul expressed his own views on the sinfulness of every man and the abyss of darkness which lies hidden, always, in each one of us. This can be overcome only by the power of God but it can emerge again at any moment if it is not continually under God's control. And when we refuse or neglect God's power, what Paul calls 'sin personified' comes back to the surface.

To reflect on the darkness in man's heart is not merely to meditate on something far away from us but on something which is really in us, or rather lies in wait within us. The sad experience of each one of us tells us that this 'lying in wait' can sometimes be changed quickly and unexpectedly into reality. This is an unpopular subject which it is hard to discuss in everyday language.

We tend to swing continually between two positions. On the one hand, we sometimes deplore man's evil when we see disturbing events. I refer to violence, the cruelties of terrorism or even of prison, where prisoners kill each other — hellish situations where people hate each other although they are undergoing the same punishment. We ourselves are horrified at some of the barbarous murders which have taken place quite recently. On the other hand, we comfort ourselves with the thought of men of good will: everyone is good at heart, every man has essential goodness.

We never really manage to get to the bottom of these two positions and to reconcile them: we move between moralizing and deploring on the one hand and a good-natured understanding for everyone on the other. We often lack the vision which would enable us to see the evil in man but with compassion and not just in a critical and pessimistic way.

What then is the extent of the shadows and darkness of which Paul writes in his letters, reflecting on all that happened to him at the time of his conversion?

We can express this on three different levels:

a) the level of *personal* sin;

b) the level of *root* sin;

c) the level of *structural* sin.

Personal sin

There are two passages which are relevant here: "Now the works of the flesh are well known: fornication, impurity, licentiousness, idolatry, witchcraft, hatred, discord, jealousy, strife, divisions, factions, envy, drunkenness, orgies and such like; of these things I warn you, as I have said before, that those who do them will not inherit the Kingdom of God" (Galatians 5:19-21). Here we are on the level of individual personal sins: it is an impressive list of the fourteen negative attitudes of man which Paul draws from his own time and experience. It is a very realistic and at the same time pessimistic view of the man who is concerned only with his own interests.

These are the works of the flesh. They are the works which come from the man who lives entirely for his own benefit. Man is then seen as a being full of "fornication, impurity, licentiousness, idolatry, witchcraft, hatred, discord . . . ". Here Paul takes a dramatic look at the society and people of his time.

The second passage paints a further picture of the same situation, listing twenty-one negative attitudes: "Because they have refused to acknowledge God, God has left them to the mercy of their own depraved minds, so that their actions are base, full of all kinds of wrong, wickedness, greed and cunning; full of envy, murder, rivalry, fraud, malice, slanderers, scandalmongers, enemies of God, spiteful, proud, boastful, inventing evil, disobedient to parents, lacking understanding, disloyal, heartless and merciless" (Romans 1:28-31). This is a description which seems perhaps rhetorical, so exaggerated is its language, but it is in fact a realistic picture of the society of his time.

Re-reading these two lists, we may ask what sort of description it is. These are social sins, that is, sins against one's neighbour: they describe the twisted way man treats his fellows, the result of a faulty knowledge of God and in the last analysis, a mistaken conception of life based on egoism.

The Apostle wishes to show the people of his day — who were just as proud as those of our own day, thinking themselves cultured and civilized with laws and a system of justice which made them vastly superior to the savages — that they are wretched, miserable men, a prey to every type of perversion because they are seeking nothing but their own personal advantage.

Paul describes things as he sees and experiences them, but he knows very well that what he describes can be found also in him. According to the basic teaching of Jesus in Mark 7:21-22: "These things come out of a man's heart". Not only from the heart of a man who happens to be born in unfortunate circumstances, but from the heart of every man.

Comparing Paul's list with that of Jesus, we can see this fundamental teaching: all these things are within us. Knowing that they are within us encourages us to take them much more seriously and to think carefully about them. Let us think for example of an item which appears in both lists: envy. Or discord, divisions, factions. How true it is that these are things we harbour in our own hearts! Clement of Rome believes that Paul was killed out of envy; it was not persecution, the wickedness of the pagans, but the envy of certain men, his rivals, who denounced him.

This means that the Christian community was subject to strife, rivalry, divisions and factions and the Christians to a certain extent availed themselves of pagan help to further their own activities and vendettas. It was certainly pagan authority which carried out the persecutions but they would not have affected so many people, Paul infers, if the Christians themselves had been more united.

The death of Peter himself has been attributed to envy, to information and help given from within the circle of Jewish Christians or by rival groups.

Let us think of other items on this list: slanderers and scandalmongers — and acknowledge that we are often these when we speak of others.

If we continue to read the list, we shall find how near it is to our everyday experience and that sometimes these attitudes emerge in force simply because we have not been watchful and aware enough of the evil within us which we should continually submit to the light of God. There is nothing more harmful than the lessening of evangelical vigilance which is one of the fundamental virtues.

Even the priest who is not vigilant and stops keeping watch over himself, who thinks that a certain way of living can be maintained by mere force of habit, even he can succumb to the pressure of any one of the negative forces described by Paul which may emerge and assert themselves in his life.

These works of the flesh which we find in the Apostle's

letters served as self-examination lists for catechumens and for Christians in their practice of penance.

This level of personal sin applies to all of us, because these are things whose ill effects are immediately discernible and which are rooted in us, in the negative inclination to which every one of us is prone.

Root sin

Paul goes deeper and, following the teaching of Jesus, denounces the basic sin which is at the root of all the others: "And since they have refused to acknowledge God, God has left them to the mercy of their own depraved minds so that their actions are base" (Romans 1:28).

This is one of the aspects of the root sin to which man is prone and to which each of us is deeply inclined and inevitably attracted unless God's power does not come to our aid.

What is this root sin? It can be expressed in many ways, by each of us according to his own experience. It is the "sin" of which John speaks in the fourth Gospel, nearly always using the singular. Basically it consists in the refusal to recognize God as God, it is the sin which lies at the root of Satan's revolt: failure to recognize that our life depends entirely on God.

The root of everything that is called 'worldliness' lies here — it is a hidden root and therefore not easy to explain. It is not an inclination to evil, as for example in the man who robs, acts unjustly or tells lies. The sin lies in saying that it is unnecessary to pay heed to God, that God's Word need not determine how I live and that I alone may decide.

This is the root sin from which come all personal shortcomings, all our other sins. For Paul the fundamental distortion consists in failure to recognize the God of the Gospel; it is the tendency to deny that man is answerable to God and should live according to his Word; it is the instinctive refusal, in itself diabolical and irrational, to allow oneself to be loved and saved by God and to live by his love. This refusal can even take the form of zeal as it did in Paul's case; boasting of his tradition and moral respect-

34

ability, he was in fact denying the mercy of God as the determining factor in his life.

This is the sin which really needs to be healed in man if the roots of the works of the flesh are to be removed. Wickedness, malice, greed, spite and envy are not just frailty and weakness, their origin lies much deeper.

Man is terribly discontented with himself and his discontent comes out in contradictory and abnormal ways. This self-hatred is, basically, the refusal to be loved, to let oneself be loved; to make an absolute idol of one's independence, with all the resulting sadness or desperation and all the cruelty and injustice to which human malice can lead. This is our only explanation of the great massacres of history, some of them recent, and the ruthless killings, present and past, in times of political and social revolution, all of which give vent to man's inner desperation.

We can thank God that only rarely do we meet such extreme cases: but we do meet them, they are there and they make history. In fact, what happened in Hitler's concentration camps cannot be explained except in terms of this diabolical refusal to acknowledge God.

Paul, speaking of this sin, is distressed because in his own case and in everyone else's, he stresses that it is invincible.

"We know in fact that the Law is spiritual while I am carnal, sold into slavery to sin. And I cannot even understand the things I do: in fact I don't do what I want to do but what I hate. So, if I do what I don't want to do, I acknowledge that the Law is good; so it is no longer I who do it but the sin which lives in me. In fact I know that there is no good in me, that is, in my flesh; I have the desire to do the right thing but not the ability to put it into effect; so I do not do the good that I want to do but the bad that I don't want" (Romans 7: 14-19).

This human impotence is a historical fact; it is most mysterious and presents an almost absurd paradox. Man desires the good but he realizes that he does not do it. Conditioned by events, tensions, difficulties and opposition to be overcome, he hardens himself and by so doing he closes in on himself and his difficulties, falling into possessiveness and self-defence and thus refusing to depend on the mercy God extends to him in his Word.

In the worst cases, he is crushed and denies the transcendence of God. Alternatively, which is better, man sometimes lives in a state of dualism: in his good moments, he seems to be in touch with God's Word and then, when particularly difficult situations arise — bitterness, disappointment, hatred, conflicts, when he suffers injustice and wants to retaliate — he defends himself tooth and nail, opposing others and above all utterly refusing to refer to God's Word.

When Paul spoke of "the sin which lives in me", he put his finger on the deepest misery of man which is hard to understand but observable in its effects and consequences in human history.

Structural sin

This is the condition of man in history who, in fact, becomes closed in on himself because of life's hardships and against his will becomes greedy and unjust, eager to protect his own interests at all costs. This is obviously not only the result of individual malice but of culture in the wide sense of the society in which man lives out his life. It is the sin inherent in various ways of life, mental outlooks and traditional ideas; it is the general life-style which Scripture calls 'worldly' in a negative sense, in which, in spite of fine words, men seek their own advantage and feel the need to dominate others, to retaliate, to argue always rather than submit. We did not choose this state of conflict but it is a fact that we cannot escape it.

We cannot deny the truth of Paul's very dramatic analysis of the human condition; if we think it over carefully we will see that we ourselves are conditioned by it. Many of the ideas we have always accepted as obvious are the fruit of this mentality, many of our instinctive choices also stem from it. When we examine past history and wonder at the choices men have made, even in the Church — such as torture and warfare — we must understand that these people lived according to traditional ideas. It was practically impossible for them to escape the sort of outlook which led them to commit injustice. It is part of man's historical progress to be subject to the mentality of one's own time and to make inadvertent choices which one or two centuries later will be seen to have been mistaken; today, however, we make these choices quite instinctively.

It is this structural sin, inherent in social life, economics and mental outlook, which Paul denounces. He is right to do so for, while denouncing it, he affirms that deep in men's hearts there is a completely different outlook: openness to God.

Man was open to God *before* he became deaf to his voice; however, historically speaking, it is lack of openness to God which comes out and is manifested in definite situations.

This is the salvation which God offers to us: in the fullness of encounter with Christ, we can rediscover and, by his grace and mercy, recapture the potential which lay in our original openness to God, an openness which makes for true goodness and a positive society.

Man cannot realize all this unless, first of all, he has some perception of evil. Such perception should not be a source of systematic pessimism; it is in fact the thing which enables us to form a correct idea of reality.

An example from Jesus' life will help to explain what I have said about structural sin and the way we are involved in it. It is the episode which precedes the passion: "Jesus was at Bethany in the house of Simon the Leper. While he was at table, in came a woman with an alabaster flask of very expensive perfume — genuine nard; she broke the alabaster flask and poured the ointment over his head. There were some there who thought crossly: Why all this waste of perfume? That ointment could have been sold for more than three hundred pence and given to the poor! And they were very angry with her. Then Jesus said: Let her be; why are you bothering her? She has done a good thing by me" (Mark 14:3-6).

This is a case of judging a particular action. Jesus and the woman stand alone and those around them, acting instinctively, condemn that action, being unable to understand it. It is a typical case of the force of a certain mental outlook which is transmitted from person to person and leaves no room for openness to the true prophetic nature of the action. Acting on the basis of ordinary values and from the standpoint of plain commonsense, they all turn against Jesus who remains alone.

Paul identifies with the world in experiencing this common mentality.

Paul fully experiences — in himself and in solidarity with the rest of mankind — this common outlook, when he says: "What a wretch I am! Who will set me free from this body bound for death?" (Romans 7:24). In other words: I cannot escape from the reality of this situation. And immediately he adds: "We are set free, thanks be to God, through Jesus Christ our Lord!" (Romans 7:25).

In his blindness the Apostle penetrated — beyond the scope of a normal man — to the depths of man's darkness and that is how he was able to understand the power of Christ's light and his capacity to make the world anew.

In the experience of darkness, he perceived the power of baptismal enlightenment to which he voluntarily submitted at the hand of Ananias, thus receiving in the Church and from the Church the power of salvation.

The encyclical *Dives in misericordia*, speaking of unrest and the causes of unrest, says: "It is evident that a fundamental defect or rather a whole complex of defects, a defective mechanism, is at the basis of contemporary economy and the whole of materialistic civilization and this prevents the human family from breaking free of such radically unjust situations" (no. 11). The Pope applies to the situation of the whole human family that same incapacity which Paul applied to man: I see, I want, but I cannot do it. The reality of structural sin which man already feels, deep in his being, is thus extended to the structure of society in general.

Conversion and disappointment

Let us reflect on how Paul spent the period of nearly ten years which followed the event of Damascus. If we place the Damascus encounter in about 34-35 A.D., that brings us to 45-46 A.D., which marks the start of the Apostle's first really successful mission, to Cyprus and Asia Minor.

They were ten years of obscurity and difficulty. Paul does not speak much of them, perhaps even from a certain sense of decency, for he would have to say unpleasant things about the community which had received him; here and there, however, something leaks out.

Let us then remember that he started to write some thirteen to fourteen years after the experience of Damascus, by which time he had reached a full understanding of the mystery of Christ which he had seen.

We need to understand what happened to him because it represents a typical deepening of an original conversion experience, at once painful and constructive.

Lord, you hold everything in your hands. You manifestly and powerfully sustained Paul from the moment of his conversion. You never abandoned him even at the difficult times when perhaps he did not know what was happening to him. You revealed yourself to him with merciful love even when he was on the point of forsaking the ministry. Help us to understand your mercy towards us so that we may trustingly accept your guidance, believing the providential meaning of past and present events in our lives as Christians and priests. To your glory, in the power of the Spirit, Mary and all the saints interceding for us. Amen.

In this meditation:
— First, let us read the texts;
— then let us ask ourselves what is the story we can deduce from these texts;

— thirdly, let us look at the motives behind the story;

— we shall ask ourselves what Paul went through in those ten years;

— finally, we shall end with a word about ourselves.

The texts

"He stayed for a few days with the disciples in Damascus and at once started to preach in the synagogues that Jesus was the Son of God. All those who heard him were amazed and said: But is not this the man who was raging in Jerusalem against those who invoke that Name and had come here specially to take them in chains to the high priests? Saul meanwhile grew bolder all the time and confuted the Jews of Damascus, showing that Jesus is the Christ. This went on for several days and the Jews made a plot to kill him; but their plans came to Saul's ears. They were guarding the city gates day and night in order to kill him; but the disciples took him by night and let him down from the walls in a basket. Coming to Jerusalem, he tried to join himself to the disciples but they were afraid of him, not yet believing that he was a disciple. Then Barnabas took him with him, introduced him to the apostles and told them how he had seen the Lord on his journey and the Lord had spoken to him and how he had boldly preached Jesus' Name in Damascus. So he was accepted by them and went to and from Jerusalem speaking openly in the name of Jesus, holding debates with the Greek-speaking Jews; but these tried to kill him. When the brethren heard of it, however, they took him to Caesarea and made him leave for Tarsus. Then the Church was at peace in Judaea, Galilee and Samaria" (Acts 9: 19-31).

Here we can note, with a hint of malice, even if the text does not intend it, that when Paul left for Tarsus the Church was at peace; a man who created disorder and confusion had been removed from their midst.

Another interesting text can be found in the letter to the Galatians: "When he chose me from my mother's womb . . . and was pleased to reveal his Son to me . . . without going to Jerusalem to those who were apostles before me, I went to Arabia and then returned to Damascus. Then, after three years, I went to Jerusalem to consult Cephas and was with him for two weeks; I saw none of the other apostles except James, the Lord's brother. I swear before God that what I am writing to you is true. Then I went to the regions of Syria and Cilicia, but I was not known personally to the Christian churches in Judaea; all they had heard was: the man who once persecuted us is now preaching the faith he once tried to destroy. And they glorified God because of me. After fourteen years, I went to Jerusalem again with Barnabas, taking Titus with me" (Galatians 1:15-2:1). That is another series of facts.

Another text probably corresponds to those fourteen years: "Should one boast? No, that is not right! However, I will come to visions and revelations of the Lord. I know a man in Christ, who, fourteen years ago — whether or not he was in the body, I cannot say, God knows — was taken up to the third heaven. And I know that this man — whether in the body or not, I cannot say, God knows — was taken up to the third heaven. And I know that this man — whether in the body or not, I cannot tell, God knows — was caught up to Paradise and heard unspeakable things which it is not right for a man to repeat. I will boast about him! But I will not boast about myself unless it be of my weaknesses" (2 Corinthians 12:1-5).

Paul is very reserved about describing the atmosphere of those years, but sometimes he lets himself go. As for example in the letter to the Philippians, when he finds himself in a similar situation to those he had previously experienced and says: "Be on your guard against dogs and evildoers, beware of those who get themselves circumcised! In reality, we are the 'circumcised' ones, we who worship according to the spirit of God and glory in Jesus Christ without putting our trust in the flesh, although I too could trust in the flesh" (Philippians 3:2-4). There are also some phrases in the letter to the Galatians which seem to link up with Paul's emotions at that time of his life.

The actual facts

What really happened? Various facts are fairly obvious. After his conversion, Paul starts to preach publicly, probably not always having Damascus as his base; and here is his 'stay in Arabia', perhaps in the outskirts of the city with the Arab population because his presence was not entirely welcome.

At one point the authorities get worried and set up such opposition that he is obliged to flee. We do not read that the community either supported him or urged him to come back; he was a disturbing influence, although they admired his zeal.

After this flight it is not recorded that he returned to Damascus or renewed his contacts with that particular group of disciples.

At Jerusalem it was much the same: he was not in such immediate danger as he had been at Damascus so this flight was not quite as adventurous! However, his preaching gradually attracts too much attention, the brethren grow concerned about him and send him back to his native land. In other words, he is thanked and sent away.

The two events of Damascus and Jerusalem are followed by a period of complete solitude in his own country, when he feels somewhat discouraged. We can deduce this from the fact that this period closes with the great vision of which he speaks in the second letter to the Corinthians which we can regard as a repetition of the Damascus vision of Christ. The new vision of God's glory, which he had perhaps been tempted to doubt, marks the close of a period of bitterness and solitude.

To sum up, the ten years from his first conversion were years of difficulty, of clashes and uneasiness caused by his over-fiery preaching methods and his taking too many risks. They were also years of lonelines, silence and discouragement.

When Paul records these things, he is looking at them from the standpoint of his second ministry and so he no longer lingers over them.

It is interesting to note this sequence of fourteen years which is repeated twice. The first period of fourteen years extends from his conversion to his second visit to Jerusalem.

The second fourteen-year period is the one referred to in 2 Corinthians between the time of the vision and the time at which he is writing the letter. When he was writing, his life seemed to him like two sabbatical periods.

In fact the Hebrews at that time used to measure time and events according to a seven-year cycle which corresponded to the period which ended with the sabbatical year.

Twenty-eight years after his conversion, Paul discerned a sacred rhythm in his life: he had already seen what had happened to him in a providential light and he realised immediately that this coincided with the sacred reckoning of time. But while he was going through the intervening periods, he could not yet fully understand why his life should have developed in such a way.

So the story of the ten years after Damascus, when Paul was between thirty and forty years of age, can be briefly stated like this: hardship at Damascus, incomprehension at Jerusalem, times of loneliness and discouragement.

The motivation behind the facts

Let us ask ourselves: during this time was there something wrong with Paul or did all the fault lie with the other people who opposed him, failed to understand and defend him and preferred to get rid of him, being unable to recognize his true worth? Probably, as in every human situation, there were faults on both sides.

It is true that the Jewish Christians above all, who were tied to a very narrow vision of the apostolate and had many fears and reservations, did not understand him and did not appreciate him because they were afraid that his activities would do more harm than good. Then the enemies of Christianity attacked him because they sensed that he was a key-figure. Between these two groups, there was a tacit agreement about Paul and together they managed to eliminate him for a while.

Besides all this, however, I think that Paul himself, if asked, would confess that there was something not quite right about him. What happened to him was what frequently happens in the case of a total and rapid conversion when everything appears in the best and most favourable light and the motive behind the conversion is not a change of camps or allegiance but the vision of new life offered in Jesus: something completely new happens, which is the work of God.

But when one tries to take up one's daily life, one is left with the same personality and Paul throws himself into the new mission with the same enthusiasm with which he had attacked the old one; he transfers his zeal from one camp to another and goes back to embracing the work as if it belonged to him.

At this point the Lord permits a time of very hard and testing purification so that he may learn that conversion has not merely made him change his field of activity but has given him a new way of life, a new way of looking at things, and he must, as it were, steep himself in this new outlook before it becomes part of his personality.

His ideas and words were clear enough; but his instinctive behaviour was still the same as it had been before.

By interpreting the facts in this way, perhaps we are speaking more about ourselves than about Paul. As we go forward in our quest for God, we are always seeking a deeper clarification of our motives, but we know all too well that this does not mean an immediate change in our instinctively possessive approach to things and situations. This possessiveness is transferred from the material to the spiritual plane, from economic to spiritual gains and we find that we are still ourselves, always needing continual purification quite apart from the words we speak or the fine ideas we express.

Paul's own experience

At this point we can ask Paul: how did you live through those ten years? What did it mean to you, this trial of loneliness, having to live on the fringe of the community? What did you think about when you went for a solitary evening walk by the river in Tarsus, where no one knew you and your thoughts kept returning to the Damascus road? What was it like to preach those first sermons at Jerusalem when you felt such a stranger among those people, so much so that at one point you almost believed the whole thing had been a dream? How did you live through that dramatic experience?

First of all, Paul reminds us that he was not the first to have this experience.

Many centuries before, Moses, hounded out of Egypt and forgotten by his own people, had gone through a similar desert experience. Elijah, too, felt abandoned by everyone and fled into the desert, terribly alone.

Speaking of his own feeling, Paul tells us that his first reaction was certainly indignation, resentment and the desire for revenge. Why waste your energy and life on people who treat you badly, on a Church and so-called brothers who don't want to know you? It is a resentment which builds up inside him, robbing him of peace and finally — as always happens — it is directed towards God as well. Why did Christ call me so insistently only to reduce me to working in my shop in Tarsus with no future prospects? Has God really got a plan for my life or are these just past dreams? What was the meaning of those words which resounded in my ears [the words which he will repeat in his speech before Agrippa]: "I have appeared to you to make you a minister and witness of those things which I will reveal to you later. For this reason I will deliver you from the people and from the Gentiles" (Acts 26:16-17). Resentment against God comes from difficulty in accepting his providence and the mysterious and incomprehensible methods of divine action.

We can be quite sure that at times Paul felt like this. The saints go through this sort of thing. No saint has been spared this interior travail so nor was the Apostle. But after the anger and resentment, when, in God's plan, one is totally immersed in temptation, there comes a time of reflection and a little question takes shape — little, but large enough to penetrate the darkness of a leaden sky: "Perhaps God's providence is saying something to me even in this?" While reading this passage from Job — ch. 5 vv. 17-20 — it struck me that such a question may indeed have come into Paul's mind, very gradually taking effect, rather like a medicine. "Happy the man whom God corrects: so do not despise the correction of the Almighty, for he will wound you and bind up the wound, he will strike you and heal you. He will save you from six tribulations and the seventh will not harm you; in time of famine he will save you from death and in wartime he will save you from the sword".

Paul who certainly read and re-read the Scriptures, was given the medicine of God's Word which acts as a balm, liberating and consoling.

As he listened again to God's Word, Paul's reflection became enlightenment and he entered once more into that bright revelation which he had had on the Damascus road. We can see this from two lines of thought which appear in his letters.

a) The first is an *eschatological meditation* which he develops in 1 Corinthians: "Brothers, time is short; from now on, those who have wives should live as if they had none; those who mourn as if they did not weep and those who are joyful as if they did not rejoice; those who buy as if they had no possessions; those who use this world without abusing it" (1 Corinthians 7 : 29ff). Paul re-directs his passionate zeal, realizing that he had been concentrating on more immediate projects whereas the Kingdom of God is beyond and above such things; that even the best and most absorbing things pass away but the Lord remains forever.

b) A second line of thought concerns *enlightenment*: it is God's work: it is God who lays down times and conditions. Paul takes a second step in detachment from self. The first was when he left behind his privileges as a Pharisee and a Hebrew and son of Hebrews. The second step in detachment involves losing the things he could have been justly proud of: his ease in preaching the Word in

46

persuasive, fiery and violent language, vastly superior to the timid approach of the others in Jerusalem.

Paul understands the importance of all these things but it is the Lord's work: "Who are you to be judging another man's servant? It is in his master's eyes that he stands or falls" (Romans 14:4). We think things ought to go a certain way, but it is the Lord who has the work in hand: "What is Apollos? What is Paul?" (1 Corinthians 3:5). And he goes on: "We are ministers through whom you have come to the faith according to the Lord's gift to each. I planted, Apollos watered but the Lord made the seed grow. There is no difference between the one who plants and the one who waters, but each will be rewarded for his own work. We are in fact co-workers with God and you are God's field, God's building" (1 Corinthians 3:5-9). You are not 'my' field, 'my' building: it is God's building.

Through painful experience, Paul comes to realize the very simple truth that God is Lord and that God's minister must prepare himself by emptying his heart of all personal achievements so that he may become more and more a versatile instrument in the hands of God.

In the vision of the third heaven described in 2 Corinthians, the Apostle understands things which we do not know because he did not wish to describe them. Certainly he becomes aware of the absolute and indescribable transcendence of the mystery of God which had come so close to him in the vision of Christ that he had thought to possess it — whereas in reality it is beyond human power to speak of it or dispose of it.

It is at this point that Barnabas arrives in Tarsus with the news that a young Christian community in Antioch would like to have him. Barnabas suggests going with him to start the work. This is the second phase of his apostolic work. He now resumes, in a new way, what he had started ten years before with so much zeal but also with so much of self. In the mysterious designs of God, all that had had to pass through the fire of purification.

A question to ask ourselves

Having sought to interpret what happened to Paul during his exile in Tarsus, let us ask ourselves a last question: who is the object of our zeal? It is difficult to answer because zeal is fundamental to the work of the apostolate; the word itself means something that 'devours' and 'involves' a man. Just because we are so involved, we run the risk of becoming possessive.

— When did we have our second conversion?

— Have there been times in our lives at which our first conversion — that first, peaceful realization of our incorporation into Christ in family or parish, which we cannot perhaps fix at a precise moment — has this first conversion been put to the test in some particularly difficult experience which has made us sift our attitudes and discover a certain 'apostolic possessiveness'?

— Since God called us to a second conversion, what has been the quality of our zeal?

True zeal is something which deeply involves us without being personal. If we are rejected or fail to find the outlet we want, this should not become a personal problem which causes depression and discouragement and brings us to the end of our resignation and abandonment to God's will.

All this happens, nearly always, because we are made in such a way that we cannot throw ourselves into a thing without being involved in it and we cannot be involved in actual fact unless we put our whole being into it on both a personal and psychological level. We cannot experience events in which God is clearly at work without being affected, sometimes painfully so. But that is just where Providence awaits us — and not in order to rebuke us. If Paul went through these trials, we are not better men than he was. If he felt himself involved on his own account, the same will happen to us. We are not told not to expect such a time: rather we are told that it is a providential moment, a time for the revelation of the mystery of God, that mystery which is the vision of Christ on the road to Damascus.

48

We are not asked to be invulnerable but to open our eyes to the merciful designs of God. As Paul was led by a merciful path, so it will be for us: in all the difficulties, great and small, which our apostolic involvement brings, there is a word of mercy and salvation.

Job's words: "God wounds and heals" prove that the Lord loves us and purifies us because he wants us to possess that inner freedom which will fit us to be true servants of the Gospel.

Let us ask for the prayers of Mary. May she who from the beginning was free of heart, but had to perfect that freedom through suffering, ask the Lord to help us to pass through our trials without changing or diminishing or losing our own inner freedom. May the Lord purify us and may we be ready, like Paul, to respond freely to the new call to preach at Antioch.

Priestly examination of conscience

In the light of our meditations so far, let us now take a brief look at the new penitential rite. It falls into three parts:
— "confessio laudis"
— "confessio vitae"
— "confessio fidei".

Confessio laudis. This means starting the confession with an act of thanksgiving, answering the question: What should I chiefly thank God for at this time?

Confessio vitae. This should answer the question: Before God, what is there in my life that I would wish undone? What weighs most heavily on me at this moment? The answer should cover omissions as well as interior attitudes arising from such omissions: antipathy, resentment, suspicion, disappointment, bitterness; all things which perhaps are not specific sins but which ordinarily lead to sin. If we humbly place these before God and the Church, we open ourselves to the healing work of grace.

Confessio fidei. This is the assurance that God in his love accepts and heals me. The act of sorrow then becomes an act of faith.

This meditation, entitled 'Priestly examination of conscience', will be a last consideration of the nineteen years following Paul's conversion. It will give us plenty of material to prepare ourselves for sacramental confession.

Lord Jesus, you know how much we want to serve you and how we feel impelled by the Spirit to the work of the pastorate. You know that often in the course of our service we are assailed by doubts and fears and we wonder if what we are doing is really important, and if we are doing it in the best way. We ask you, Lord Jesus, chief Shepherd of the Church's flock, bishop of our souls, to enlighten us so that in all things we may imitate you as Shepherd and Paul as shepherd of your flock. Heal our hearts of all that disturbs them and prevents them from understanding the words of the Apostle. Help us to forget our miseries so that we may understand with open hearts the meaning of those words and the truths of love and salvation which they hold for us. You see that we are unable to understand and express these truths unless you enlighten our spirits, our minds and our words. We ask you this, Lord Jesus, who with the Father and the Holy Spirit live and reign forever and ever. Amen.

Let us take as our starting-point the first phrases of Paul's speech at Miletus. This speech corresponds somewhat to what we are doing in this series of meditations. Long before us, the evangelist Luke in the book of Acts, referring to Paul's words at Miletus, tried to recall the points which the Apostle would have had particularly in mind while recording his own past relationship to a community.

This speech, which is also called 'Paul's pastoral testament' or 'farewell speech', is an unrivalled masterpiece.

As a farewell speech it is akin to many similar farewell speeches which the Scriptures give us: chapter 49 of Genesis with Jacob's farewell speech to his sons; Deuteronomy with Moses' farewell speech; the last two chapters of Joshua, 23 and 24, with the testament of Joshua; and the same applies to Samuel, David, Tobias, Mattathias. Jesus himself at the Last Supper (John 13-17) makes a long farewell speech which is also a restrospective look at his life. Paul's speech stands in this tradition.

It is interesting to note that the New Testament gives only two farewell speeches: those of Jesus and Paul. Thus it emphasizes the importance of these two figures.

From the point of view of linguistic analysis, Paul's testament is on an I-you basis: I have been with you . . . you know; I am going to Jerusalem . . .; you will never see my face again.

This is not the sort of language Paul usually uses; in

his speech at Antioch in Pisidia, he always spoke about God and what God had done. This is precisely what makes the speech at Miletus a pastoral address in which Paul reflects on the relationship between him and those whom he has been leading for three years in the ways of God.

So it is most suitable as a priest's examination of conscience. Here we see the things Paul thought important and which had been characteristic of his behaviour towards the community. Bearing this in mind, let us attempt a deeper understanding of the speech. Being unable to meditate on the whole speech, I will confine myself to the analysis of the first verse, using a very fine book, *The Pastoral Testament of Paul* by Jacques Dupont. It is a most valuable and thoughtful commentary on this basic New Testament pastoral text.

Dupont's line of approach is very simple: he takes each word and weighs it up slowly and carefully in the light of Paul's life and of similar affirmations to be found in his letters. In this way one can understand the speech as a synthesis of Paul's pastoral teaching and his way of relating to a community.

The verse we will consider in detail: "I have served the Lord in all humility, with many tears" (Acts 20:19), stresses an important pastoral attitude for the Church in all ages.

"To be with"

With the introductory words of the speech, Paul refers briefly to his three-year ministry in Ephesus: "You know how I have been with you all the time since the first day I came to Asia". He refers to it in such a way as to throw the ball into his hearers' court at once. He does not need to begin by describing himself; he refers to the experience others have had of him.

Reading these introductory words we understand that Paul feels at one with his community, he feels that he is known, a familiar figure. He does not have to recount anything because "You know, you have seen me, I have been with you". His ministry can be summed up like this: "He is someone who has been among the people", someone whom people know, about whom everyone knows and can bear witness.

It is a ministry based on 'being with', on communicating and living with people. Paul knows very well that they looked to him for an example and he feels an absolute responsibility not only for the words he has spoken but for what he has done. Not "You remember what I've told you in these years — " but "You know what I have done". The people looked at the sort of person he was, and how he lived. This was much more important to them than whether his words were interesting, beautiful, true or practical.

And what he did was to serve.

"I have served the Lord"

His activity in the community is described like this: "I have served the Lord with tears in all humility". To serve the Lord is the first reality. Paul sees himself and he knows that others see him first of all as a servant of Christ and not as a servant of the community. This qualification characterizes his attachment to Christ and his freedom vis-a-vis the community. We sometimes speak of the ministry as a 'service' and we mean the service of the Church, the diocese, the people. The New Testament speaks of service and servants in relationship to Jesus Christ. It is true that Paul sometimes says: "I am your servant for Christ's sake" (Galatians 15:13), but usually it is "the servant of Christ".

So the pastor should live primarily in service of the person of Christ. Only in this way can he serve the Church, the people, the nation.

Paul's liberty of spirit is amazing: he owes nothing to anyone but Christ; and through him, therefore, he owes it to everyone. He need please no one and respond to no one but Christ and the community knows very well that he is not there to please, to make people happy and to fulfil their expectations but he is there to serve Christ.

"With tears"

If we had had to finish the sentence ourselves, we would have added: with zeal, fervour, intelligence, courage, competence, perseverance.

His experience makes him say different things: "with tears, in all humility". We are amazed that he should stress such a negative aspect and we ask why.

Undoubtedly we must take into account that this is a farewell speech. It is not a farewell which will take him on to an important new mission. What clearly awaits him is persecution and suffering. It is a most nostalgic address and quite naturally recalls past sufferings and anticipates future ones.

But apart from this it needs to be said that if humility and tears emerge as a way of serving God, it means that this was Paul's experience, that the things which stood out in his life were humility, tears, trials, dangers and difficulties.

He presents himself as he feels himself to be; the Apostle would be deceiving us, in this case, if he were to stress elements which were not in fact representative of his state of mind and heart.

Let us try to think carefully about his apostolic activity in Ephesus so that we may reach a better understanding of his humility and tears. He mentions tears on many other occasions: it is a recurrent theme in the Miletus speech and in his letters. It can be found again in Acts: "Be watchful, remembering that for three years, night and day, I have not ceased to exhort you with tears". These are tears shed in the affectionate, loving and persistent effort to convince someone.

From the letters we can quote: "I have written to you at a time of great sorrow, in anguish of heart and with many tears" (2 Corinthians 2:4). Tears are an extreme experience for Paul. He does not seem to have been a man readily given to tears, yet he found himself in situations of such tension and extreme difficulty, such bitterness and disappointment, that he broke down either while speaking or writing to people.

All this shows that the emotional intensity with which Paul exercised his pastoral ministry was considerable. The exact opposite of the civil servant, office worker or intelligent programmer.

Paul is a man of intense emotions, who is evidently capable of deep joy as well. Just because he entered so deeply into the sufferings of his ministry, he could also experience the glorious joy and enthusiasm of which he speaks even more frequently in his letters. He wrote: "How can we thank God for you, for all the joy we feel before God because of you?" (1 Thessalonians 3 : 9).

The intense sufferings are compensated for by very deep joys and extraordinary enthusiasm: "I have great confidence in you and I am very proud of you. I am full of consolation and joy in the midst of all our tribulations" (2 Corinthians 7 : 4). I am so pleased with you that I no longer feel my sufferings when I think of your letters, your affection and your faith. We all know what these experiences mean: he who loves greatly also suffers and rejoices greatly; he who loves little suffers and rejoices less.

In these first lines, Paul gives us the picture of a pastor as a man who is deeply involved, both affectively and emotionally, in what he is doing. He has a deep love for people, a personal love: he remembers individual names and personal details about family circumstances, work or illness. He sees these Christians as individuals, each one being either a source of bitterness, sadness and tears or of intense joy.

That is the sense in which he served the Lord with tears.

"In all humility"

Here, too, we need to understand why, among the thousand other ministerial qualifications, Paul should have chosen this one, emphasizing it as a fundamental pastoral attitude.

The Greek term can mean "in all kinds of humiliation", referring not to the attitude but to various situations. This is the meaning in the *Magnificat* when Mary says: "The Lord has looked on the humility of his servant". It means insignificance, abjection, littleness and worthlessness and not the virtue of humility. But whereas in the *Magnificat* the Greek word is 'tapeinosis', here it is 'tapeinofrosune': the sense of humility. Paul is referring here to the attitude of humility with which he has served the Lord in his pastoral work.

Humility is a word we very often say but it is not often easy to grasp all the implications it has for the Apostle.

In a general sense we could say that humility is the opposite of what is described in the *Magnificat*: "God has scattered those who were proud at heart". The proud are those who think they are somebody, who are so conceited that they live only for themselves, expecting to be served by others and rarely thanking those others for service which they consider to be their due. This is the attitude which Paul criticizes elsewhere in his letters, for example when he is writing to the Romans: "Do not aspire to things which are too high for you but rather humble yourselves. Do not have too high an opinion of yourselves" (Romans 12:16). To have a humble attitude is to avoid boasting and self-deception.

It is important to reflect on this attitude of not knowing: it is always useful but in one's relationship with God it is indispensable. In fact, "we do not even know how to pray, we do not know what to ask for" (cf. Romans 8:26).

We often fail to pray well because we assume that we know how to pray whereas we should always start by confessing: "Lord, I do not know how to pray; I know I don't know!" This is already a prayer because it leaves room for the Spirit whom we should always invoke.

Humility as a characteristic attitude of Paul's pastoral activity can be viewed from three different aspects:
— the social aspect: a way of behaving;
— the personal aspect: a certain self-knowledge;
— the theological aspect: a certain relationship to God.

a) *The social aspect* means being *undemanding for oneself* and also *concerned for others*. Paul would say: "I have tried to be undemanding when I was with you, not asking for special treatment, but being very concerned for each one of you".

He describes himself like this in the first letter to the Thessalonians as he takes a backward glance at his relationship to the community: "As God found us worthy to be entrusted with the Gospel, we preach it, not so as to please men, but God, who searches our hearts. In fact, we have never uttered words of flattery, as you know, nor have thought of our own gain: God is our witness. Never have we sought human glory from you or others nor have we stood on our authority as apostles of Christ. Instead, we have been gentle among you, like a mother feeding and caring for her own children. Loving you in this way, we would gladly have given you, not only the Gospel of God but our very lives, so dear were you to us" (1 Thessalonians 2 : 4-8).

Humility, undemanding friendship, extreme affection and care, gentleness and thoughtfulness. Paul feels that, by the grace of God, he has shown all this and that his way of life should be a model for each pastor. Humility as a social virtue also includes a certain distinction, propriety and reserve, thoroughly good manners, the priestly finesse which wins men's hearts because it is more than mere outward affectation. For those who know that they are little esteemed socially, there is nothing more touching than to be treated with extreme respect and appreciation of what they are. Paul's converts were for the most part slaves, used to being badly treated, teased, despised, neglected, and we can imagine what it meant to them to feel respected and sincerely loved. How astonished they must have been by Paul's apostolic methods!

b) *The personal aspect* is a simple judgment on oneself. Paul comes back several times to this ability to make a right judgment of oneself, achieving self-understanding through our own weaknesses and frailties. In the first letter to the Corinthians, he speaks of Jesus' apparition to him: "After all the rest, he appeared to me also. I am the least of the apostles, I am not worthy to be called an apostle" (1 Corinthians 15:8-9). He says this truthfully and sincerely: it is not an affectation but an accurate judgment of himself.

And this judgment is one which he has arrived at in the school of life which had taught him his own frailty and poverty. He has learned to think of himself with humility and detachment, calmly and peacefully, without self-condemnation. "Indeed we do not want you to be unaware, brothers, that the trouble which we had in Asia quite overwhelmed us; it was quite beyond our strength, so that we even despaired of life itself. But we have received the death sentence to teach us not to trust in ourselves but in the God who raises the dead" (2 Corinthians 1:8-9). We are amazed, almost scandalized, by an apostle who speaks of himself in this way.

It is difficult for a young man to have personal humility as this virtue usually grows with one's experience of life. He may perhaps have meditated on these things but they do not come naturally to him because he has not passed through the school of trials and experiences of his own weakness which keep us in our place and free us from all presumption.

It is sad to see how sometimes we go through these trials without profiting by them. If Paul, faced by the troubles which came upon him in Asia, had started to curse everyone and everything, instead of acknowledging his own weakness and frailty, he would have gained nothing by his trial. Instead, he became a true pastor just because he was able to come through that particular sorrow to a real humility which he subsequently expressed in his life.

c) *The theological aspect.* Paul expresses himself in this way because he has a deep realization of his true worth before God: "Who then gave you this privilege? What have you ever possessed that you have not received? And if you have received it, why boast as if you had not received it?" (1 Corinthians 4:7). The foundation of his attitude of humility, which was one of the secrets of his ability to win men's hearts, was a strong sense of God as creator. lord and master, the merciful giver of all good things. Before him, Paul is a poor sinner who receives grace, mercy and salvation. The very Word is the Word of God, not Paul: it has been given to him, according to the measure of the gift of Christ. Paul's very apostolic zeal is not his own but has been given him by Christ who lives within him.

This humility is a reflection of the divine indwelling, a Christological reflection, of Christ as he has known and understood him, Christ the Servant of Yahweh, Christ humble and humiliated, who did not choose to shine by throwing himself off the pinnacle of the Temple and causing a sensation, by changing stones into bread, by ruling over the kingdoms of the world, but chose to be the servant of all.

Paul's humility is the humility he received from Christ and which he expresses by letting Christ live within him.

This is why Paul can describe humility as the basic attitude of one who serves the Lord, as the Lord has served. Christ served in all humility and his servant chooses the same way, exercising authority with the humility, gentleness and meekness of the Master. This is certainly one of the radical distinctions between pastoral and political power. Pastoral power is founded on the gentleness of Christ and this is precisely why, as in Paul's case, it can also take the form of hard, cutting and resolute speech or writing; this is not with a view to self-defence but in order to demonstrate the meekness and humility of Christ in the face of the realities of life.

Each one of us should meditate deeply on these things, knowing how very far we are from this ideal. Our own personality instinctively comes to the fore each time it is a question of exercising power and we are constantly tempted to mix the service of the Lord with our personal prestige.

We need to follow the Apostle's example and be purified, above all by the power of Christ within us. Let us ask Mary whom the Lord preserved in humility, to pray that we may follow Christ as Paul did, knowing that it is an arduous task and that we are far from our goal.

By the grace of God let us try to face this, acknowledging our shortcomings and asking that the power of Christ, alive in us, may make us like him.

Conversion and estrangement

Let us reflect on another obscure and very dramatic episode in Paul's life: the estrangement and break with Barnabas.

In the last moments of his life, Paul, thinking over the times which most upset him, would probably not have thought particularly of the imprisonments, persecutions, shipwrecks, the thirty-three strokes of the lash, in fact, the items listed in 2 Corinthians 11. Nothing seems to have marked him quite as much as this event.

Paul does not speak of it in his letters. This episode, which is difficult for us to interpret, forms part of those dark times through which the man of God passes in order to be refined and purified.

Let us ask God in prayer to open the eyes of our hearts so that we may understand the significance of those obscure events in the life of the early Church, in the Church of all times and in our own lives.

Lord Jesus, you know that we experience so many things that are hard to understand and we see around us, in the history of the Church and of your saints, so many happenings whose meaning we do not fully grasp. Lord, we do not ask to understand but we do ask to be able to love more, we would like to draw from what we can understand, the capacity to love, for we are sure that nothing can separate us from the power of the Spirit which is poured out in our hearts.

May the power of the Spirit be present in us now as we read the Scriptures.

Mary, Mother of God, grant that if we cannot understand, we may at least love. All this we ask of God the Father, source of light and love who overcomes all darkness through Christ the light of the world, through the Spirit, the light who enlightens our night. Amen.

61

Let us ask ourselves:
— First of all, who was Barnabas?
— then, what was Barnabas to Paul?
— what happened?
— and what were the consequences?
— how did Paul experience this traumatic separation?

Who was Barnabas?

He was one of the giants of the early Church, one of the very first to take the Gospel seriously. He had probably not known the Lord but he was of such merit that Peter, Andrew, James and John, who had been with the Lord, had confidence in him.

He was one of the first to believe the apostles' preaching, one of the first to offer himself, the first to sell all his possessions. He is introduced to us in Acts: "Joseph, whom the apostles surnamed Barnabas, which means 'son of exhortation', a Levite from Cyprus who owned some land, sold it and laid the proceeds at the feet of the apostles" (Acts 4:36). At a time when the community hardly amounts to anything, being a meagre band of men, possibly fanatics, he believed, he sold everything and wholeheartedly took the part of the apostles and Christ. Because of this, he is called 'son of exhortation, son of consolation'.

As a personality, Barnabas was a man rich in wisdom and optimism, he radiated confidence and others willingly went with him and trusted in him.

In fact we see him being used in the most important missions. His name appears again in chapter 11 of Acts: when it is a question of finding out what is happening in Antioch, they sent Barnabas from Jerusalem. Barnabas goes to Antioch and "when he came and saw the grace of God, he was glad and, being a virtuous man, full of the Holy Spirit and faith, he exhorted them all to cling resolutely to the Lord" (Acts 11:23-24).

Barnabas is the man who could recognize the authenticity of the Christianity of Western Greece and Asia Minor.

Without him, who knows how long the Church would have remained tied to the ideas of the Jewish Christians in Jerusalem? Barnabas is a man of profound intuition, he is free of prejudice and fear and understands that the Spirit is at work in Antioch. He can also act as mediator: to reassure Jerusalem and encourage Antioch, avoiding a split between the two. So he is a man of great value to primitive Christianity.

What Barnabas was to Paul

He was of the first importance; after Ananias he is the man to whom Paul owes most. In fact he owes his Christian initiation and original acceptance to Ananias but then he owes all the rest to Barnabas. What he did for Paul was to look for him (we mentioned him when speaking of the sad period in Tarsus); he understood him and supported him. He was a friend, spiritual father and teacher in the apostolate, the one who introduced him to his first apostolic experience.

Let us look at some texts. After fleeing from Damascus, Saul goes to Jerusalem: "He tried to join the apostles, but they were all afraid of him, not yet believing that he was a disciple" (Acts 9:26). The mistrust which had arisen between Jerusalem and Antioch is present here in Jerusalem with regard to this new arrival who doesn't seem to know what he wants. The text goes on: "Barnabas took with him and introduced him to the apostles and told them how during the journey he had seen the Lord who had spoken to him and how in Damascus he had boldly preached in the name of Jesus" (Acts: 9:27).

It is an excellent thing to comment on this text word by word: "Barnabas took him with him": the Greek verb is 'epilabomenos', the same which is used when Jesus takes Peter's hand when he is about to sink in the lake during the storm (cf. Matthew 14:31). We can picture to ourselves a bewildered Paul in Jerusalem: doors are shut in his face, he hasn't even a place to sleep, and Barnabas

63

comes along, takes him by the hand and says: "Come with me, I'll go with you and introduce you".

It is through Barnabas that the doors are opened again to Paul. Acts tells us: "So he was able to stay with them and he went to and from Jerusalem speaking openly in the name of the Lord" (Acts 9:28).

And later, when we hear of the Antioch community, Barnabas is the first of the prophets: "In the community at Antioch there were prophets and teachers: Barnabas, Simeon surnamed Niger, Lucius of Cyrene and Manaan who has been brought up with Herod the tetrarch, and Saul" (Acts 13:1). So the people of Antioch recognize the prophets, but the first is Barnabas and Saul is the latest arrival, and we know how "Barnabas then went to Tarsus to look for Saul and when he had found him he brought him to Antioch. They stayed together in that community for a whole year and taught many people; at Antioch the disciples were called Christians for the first time" (Acts 11:25-26).

Behind this last verse we catch a glimpse of a marvellous collaboration between Barnabas and Paul: Barnabas is the first of the prophets, Paul the latest arrival, but Barnabas sees his true worth and introduces him to a work which is to become the most fruitful in the whole early Church; it is at Antioch that the Christian faith takes such a hold that the very name 'Christian' comes from that town. It is a community which really made its mark in history.

Barnabas was all this to Paul.

Barnabas is also the first chosen by the Spirit for the mission. There is a description of the start of the mission which will later become the great mission to the pagans: "While these men — the prophets — were worshipping the Lord and fasting, the Spirit said: Let me have Barnabas and Saul for the work to which I have called them" (Acts 13:2). Barnabas is the first and Saul is his assistant. Barnabas is the leader of the new expedition; describing it, the author always mentions Barnabas first. The order is always significant: Barnabas is the one who is officially recognized as leader of the mission: in verse 7 it says that they met the proconsul, a wise man "who sent for Barnabas and Saul and wanted to hear the word of God".

It is during this mission that we can observe a very rapid emergence of Paul's personality. A few verses later, we see that Saul is the chief actor in the drama when Elymas the Sorcerer is blinded: 'Saul, also called Paul, full of the Holy Spirit, looked at him steadily and said: O man full of deceit and all kinds of wickedness" (Acts 13:9); and further on: "Having left Paphos, Paul and his companions came to Perga in Pamphilia" (Acts 13:13). Barnabas has already been reduced to the rank of 'companion'.

We can observe here the gradual psychological change and the reversal of roles which took place on this early expedition.

And unfortunately, after a short time, when the reversal of roles has already been more or less accepted — the first sermon of the mission in Acts 13 is attributed to Paul, not Barnabas: "Paul rose and beckoning to them, said: Men of Israel . . . " (Acts 13:16) — it happens that John Mark goes off and the expedition is reduced in number.

During the whole of the first missionary journey, Barnabas and Paul take alternate turns at leadership.

In the episode at Lystra, when the pagans see the healing of the paralytic and mistake the two missionaries for divine beings, the text reads: "They called Barnabas Zeus and Paul Hermes" (Acts 14:12). In this case Barnabas was seen as the old man, the bearded ancient, while Paul was the active and enterprising one, the spokesman. So the roles were divided and the people regarded first one and then the other as the leader: "Hearing this, the apostles Barnabas and Paul tore their clothes and rushed into the crowd crying: Good people, why are you doing this?" (Acts 14:14-15). Barnabas is once again the first to be mentioned.

A short time later, there grew up radical opposition to their mission and Paul — so the text says — is stoned and thrown out of the city. It is clear that, although it is still a bit uncertain who is the real leader of the mission, Paul gradually gains prominence in the eyes of the people. The mission ends without disaffection apart from the incident of Mark's departure which grieves the two missionaries, but does not cause difficulties for the time being.

The next chapter, Acts 15, shows Paul and Barnabas in the closest collaboration always, however, in this order: Paul and then Barnabas. The two are in complete agreement and co-operate fully, sharing together the task of resisting the injunctions of the Judaizers to circumcise the pagan converts. The whole of chapter 15 reveals full collaboration between the two.

What happened?

Towards the end of chapter 15 comes the drama of the division between them.

The Council of Jerusalem has just taken place. The letter has been consigned to Paul, Barnabas and two other brothers, Judas Barsabbas and Silas, who are to take it to Antioch. Going up to Antioch, they remain there to teach and preach the Word of God and then Paul decides to carry on with the mission. Let us read the text: "After some days Paul said to Barnabas: Let us go back and visit the brothers in all the towns where we have preached the Word of the Lord, to see how they are doing" (Acts 15:36). It is no longer a community led by Barnabas and Saul but Paul who feels himself responsible for all the work in Asia Minor and wants to visit the brothers again. "Barnabas wanted to take John Mark with them but Paul maintained that they should not take a man who had deserted them in Pamphilia and had not wanted to take part in their work. Their disagreement was such that they separated from each other; Barnabas taking Mark with him. embarked for Cyprus. Paul took Silas instead and left, being commended by the brethren to the grace of God" (Acts 15:37-40).

What happened? At first sight the narrative is quite clear: a disagreement over a fellow-worker. It was all right with Barnabas but not with Paul. Added to this was the embarrassing fact that Barnabas was cousin of John Mark and his defence of him was probably mingled with self-love and family pride.

Paul makes a stand on a question of principle: "Their disagreement was such that they separated" (Acts 15:39). Maybe they argued for several days, perhaps the community tried to reconcile them and persuade them; but the discussion reaches such a pitch that it really seems better for each to go his own way. This climax is indicated in the Greek by the word 'paroxusmos' — paroxysm — although in other cases, it has a weaker meaning: provocation or stimulus. But in Acts 17:16 this term is used to show that Paul was furious to see the city full of idols. We can imagine Paul's fury and how very heated the argument with Barnabas became.

There is also another use of the word when Paul in the first letter to the Corinthians describes the qualities of charity: charity "ou paroxunetai" (1 Corinthians 13:5) — is not easily provoked, is not given to excessive irritation.

It is interesting to think that perhaps Paul is passing judgment on himself here, for he himself went to such an excess and was unable to restrain himself in the argument with Barnabas.

We may naturally ask ourselves if a difference of opinion about a fellow-worker could justify such a dramatic separation; or if in fact it was just a pretext. Wasn't there something more behind it? Could it not have been, from a psychological point of view, the increasing difficulty of deciding who was the leader, Paul or Barnabas? Barnabas was the man of great authority who had been known throughout the Church since the early days in Jerusalem and for that reason it was perhaps hard for him to give way to a new man, as yet unknown to many. Moreover, Paul was disliked at Jerusalem and for that reason, too, the mission might well be discredited. Or there may have been deeper psychological reasons: Barnabas was ill at ease because on the one hand, he had the responsibility and on the other, he realized that Paul, in fact, made the decisions. Paul, for his part, had the opposite difficulty. We cannot tell to what extent these elements influenced the final decision.

There is another fact: Paul was working towards a break with the Judaizers while Barnabas was on extremely good terms with the Jewish-Christian Church and thought it better not to break with them because of the grave consequences of such a move. Paul also foresaw the rift with the Jewish-Christian Church which came later and he would have liked to avoid it but in fact acted in such a way as to irritate and exasperate his opponents.

Let us also remember the incident with Peter at Antioch: Paul will write that Barnabas allowed himself to be carried away by the hypocrisy of the Jews (cf. Galatians 2:11-14).

It is impossible for us to determine the historical facts of the case. However, we must conclude that this rift was very dramatic and painful for both of them.

What were the consequences?

One of the consequences was paradoxical from the point of view of relationships. Paul who had enjoyed Barnabas' confidence and, thanks to this confidence, had been saved and put back into circulation, is unable to trust Barnabas in the question of Mark.

The suffering of Barnabas is considerable: perhaps he also feels rejected as a friend, not because of any ill will on Paul's part but as a result of the circumstances.

After this episode, Barnabas disappears. After a certain point, this giant of the early Church hardly leaves any further trace. Paul refers to him 1 Corinthians 9:6 as a well-known figure of good reputation and again, in an indirect manner, perhaps by way of reparation: "Aristarchus, my fellow-prisoner, and Mark, the cousin of Barnabas (about whom you have been given instructions; if he comes your way, give him a warm welcome)" (Colossians 4:10). Paul has been reconciled with Mark and mentioning him as

Barnabas' cousin he seems to be saying: "the one whom I once failed to welcome".

Apart from these very brief references, we know of Barnabas only from tradition. He confined himself to Cyprus, he no longer undertook great missionary journeys but, having returned to his native land, he remained there. The whole of his enormous capacity is confined within a very limited area.

Although it dates back some time, Hollzner's study *The Apostle Paul* is still a classic. Considering the various points of the narrative, the author says: "Looking at things from a human point of view, perhaps Barnabas' attitude seems kinder, while Paul seems to be harsh in his judgment of young Mark. With regard to Barnabas, too, Paul seems to be too harsh in his judgment and also unjust: he should after all have been grateful to him for having rescued him from obscurity". And further on: "His spirit had to progress to ever deeper levels of knowledge and it was by a gradual process, step by step, that his total identification with Christ was achieved". And here he quotes another German author who wrote a life of Paul and makes this comment: "Paul did not always succeed in mastering his tempestuous nature; there was only One who managed to walk this earth without gathering even a speck of its dust, and he had none of Adam's sinful nature". Then he concludes: "It is always sad when an old and sacred friendship breaks up and the firmer the bond, the more painful the separation". "How often he must have remembered the time when Barnabas was the only one who believed in him, while everyone else mistrusted him, specially the unforgettable day when he had come to Tarsus in search of him and that night at Lystra when Barnabas had bent, weeping in anguish, over the friend whom he took for dead. The heart bleeds when such bonds are broken".

Who was in the right? Time proved Barnabas to be right; but this is how things happened and from a certain point onwards each one had to adapt himself to the new situation.

We could consider one more point and think what it would have meant to the early Church if the two had not separated. Perhaps Barnabas would have acted as mediator and moderator and the Jewish-Christian Churches would not have broken off as they did. It is difficult to speculate about things that did not actually happen. Yet it is probable that, afterwards, Paul may often have regretted Barnabas' sense of moderation, his friendliness and gifts as a mediator which would have helped to clear up quite a few situations. Yet the Apostle had to go this way, without in fact having anything with which to reproach himself — or anyway very little — simply because an irritating situation had arisen without anyone realizing what was happening.

In the following years, Paul will learn to live with these difficulties and problems.

How Paul experienced the separation

Paul certainly suffered from this separation as it brought him a sense of loneliness. But this event also helped him to an even deeper understanding of what he had originally learned from the Damascus vision. The Lord is the only perfect and lifelong friend, the only one who fully understands us and never forsakes us.

Knowing Paul's affectionate and ardent spirit, we can guess how he grew in personal love for Christ, that total and very tender love which is to become ever more characteristic of him. Even today, it is astonishing to read the wonderful passages in his letters which could only have come out of struggle and suffering and an understanding that the Lord really is all. He made us and fully understands us; however great and beautiful they may be, human friendships pale in comparison with the "knowledge of Christ our Lord".

"From now on I consider everything as loss compared with the knowledge of Christ Jesus my Lord for whom I have suffered the loss of all these things which I count as so much rubbish so that I may win Christ and be found in him, not with my own righteousness derived from the Law but with the righteousness that comes from faith in Christ, that is, the righteousness which comes from God and is based on faith. So that I may know him and the power of his resurrection that I may share his sufferings, being conformed to his death, with the hope of attending the resurrection of the dead" (Philippians 3:8-11). "For me to live is Christ" (Philippians 1:21). Christ has become inseparable from him and that is why he can write to the Romans: "Who can separate us from the love of Christ?" (Romans 8:35). In the face of any possible infidelity on my part, he will still love me and call me to himself.

Through various events — not all of them clear and obvious, as we shall see — Paul is gradually led by the mercy of God to concentrate more and more on his apostolic task, seeing it as God's work, not his; he also begins to think less in terms of 'the Kingdom of God' than of 'Jesus, King and Lord'.

He gradually starts to identify the Kingdom of Christ with Christ himself: this was the laborious road along which Jesus led the apostles all his life through, and which is particularly stressed in St Mark's Gospel. In the first part, Jesus is the great healer, the wonderworker, the man whose deeds arouse enthusiasm. In the second part, the mysterious Messiah is revealed: Jesus himself is the Kingdom, Jesus in his death and resurrection is the fullness of the Kingdom.

Paul understood that the essential thing for him is Christ: all the things he does, whatever he performs, however enthusiastically he preaches, all is Christ living within him. At the root of everything else lies the fact that he is inseparable from Christ.

He is the one in whom all other friendships acquire meaning, beauty and significance. The Apostle will often return to the subject of friendship with his own people, the community, and his fellow-workers, for he certainly worked with others in spite of some difficult moments. But what he will always find best is the profound assurance which comes from this totally reliable experience: full friendship with Christ who is his life.

Let us also ask that, through the various events of our apostolic journey, our pastoral experience may emerge ever more clearly as dependence on the friendship of Christ who is our life.

The transfiguration of Paul

Starting with the historic episode of suffering in Paul's life let us meditate on the transfiguration wrought by his inner purification and then go on to think about the transfiguration of the pastor.

As we meditate, let us ask that, through our knowledge of the Apostle, we may receive the grace of the knowledge of Christ, whose glory shines from his face and would also shine on us.

We thank you, Father, for the gift of the glorious light and radiance shining from the face of your Risen Son. You have shown this glory to your Church in your servant Paul as you had shown it interiorly to Mary, Mother of Jesus, to Peter and to the apostles.

We thank you that you continue to show this glory in the history of the Church, through the saints. We thank you for the saints we have known, for all their edifying words and writings and the sustaining witness of their lives. Show the glory of Christ to us, also, so that something of that splendour may shine in us and, inwardly transformed, we may know your Son Jesus and make him known as the transforming power in the lives of all men. We ask this, Father, through Christ our Lord. Amen.

All that we have said about Paul's sufferings over the break with Barnabas can be applied to the other conflicts which marked the life of this extraordinary man: conflicts with the community, above all those referred to in 2 Corinthians and in Galatians. In these letters Paul can be seen clearly in opposition to certain sorts of behaviour; we see him in situations of tension and sorrow and loneliness. Typical of these is the conflict with Peter at Antioch in which Paul finds himself in an extremely embarrassing and difficult situation.

The first thing we must bear in mind is that we should not be surprised by these things: these conflicts arise in the history of the Church. Difficulties of collaboration between priests or between the parish priest and his assistant are of apostolic origin so we may find them already in the New Testament.

We need continually to reflect on this reality, as did Paul, in order to purify ourselves and to find a solution by going deeper into the problem and not simply resigning ourselves to it. Not to be astonished; but to grow in understanding of ourselves and others. If there were personality clashes at times in St Paul's life, how much more is this true of us. We need to be able to discern and understand that in our own conflicts it is not always a question only of the honour and glory of God but sometimes of our own personality. We need to be able to grow in compassion which is the attitude of God towards history and the realities of human life.

What is meant by transfiguration

We called this meditation 'transfiguration' because the point of reference is the transfiguration of Christ: "While he was praying, his face changed and his clothes became a glistening white" (Luke 9:29). It is interesting to note that the word used here is the same used by Luke to describe the light into which Paul enters at the time of the Damascus vision: Paul, too, stands in the reflection of the transfigured Christ.

Describing the same scene, Mark's Gospel speaks of transformation: "He was transformed, he was transfigured" (cf. Mark 9:2ff). The Greek verb is: 'metamorfothe': he was transformed, which is translated as "he was transfigured before them and his clothes became very white and resplendent". This verb is the same which Paul uses in the letter to the Corinthians to describe the process of transformation that he — and every apostle and pastor after him — experiences, reflecting the glory of Christ: "All of us [and clearly he is describing his own experience which he wants us to share] with unveiled faces, reflecting the glory of the

74

Lord as in a mirror, we are being transformed into that same image, from glory to glory by the action of the Spirit of God" (2 Corinthians 3:18).

That is a description of what we are considering: Paul, invested with the glory of the Lord at Damascus, is transformed. But the verb is in the present tense to show that it is a continual transforming action, from glory to glory by the power of the Spirit of God. He is being transformed into the image of Jesus, he is acquiring the brightness of Christ.

Let us not forget that the feast and the episode of the Transfiguration are widely used in the liturgy of the Greek Church to describe what happens in the Christian by progressive integration of the grace of baptism and, in the case of priests, the grace of ordination.

In speaking of the 'transfiguration' of Paul, I refer to the increase of light and transparency which is apparent during his life as a pastor and which can be seem most strikingly in his great letters.

Reading these letters, we are irresistibly drawn by the brilliance and splendour of his soul and after two thousand years we sense that behind the written words is a rich and vibrant personality, able to fascinate and enlighten us.

His transfigured appearance attracted people and was one of the secrets of his apostolic activity. It was the product of a long journey of trials, sufferings, incessant prayer and trust constantly renewed.

The pastor, like Paul, is called to become transparent, a source of light, and he does this by means of experience, sufferings, labours and the gifts of God.

In his words and deeds, people should be able to find that sense of peace, serenity and confidence which is indescribable but understood instinctively.

Each of us has, by the grace of God, known priests who have been like that: they radiated just as Paul did, which is very evident by the way he speaks and expresses himself generally.

Let us now try to describe it analytically so that we may compare our life as pastors with this ideal.

— In what ways is Paul a source of light?

We can discover this by looking at three inner attitudes and two more external ones which are typical of this transfiguration.

— How do we achieve and maintain in our own lives something similar to this transfiguration which is God's gift to us, too?

Inner attitudes of transfiguration

a) The first attitude, which we find in all the letters, even the most controversial, is a great inner *joy* and peace: "I am full of consolation and extremely joyful in the midst of all our troubles" (2 Corinthians 7:4). Paul clearly puts his many tribulations along with his joy, indeed a super-abundant joy. That it is neither forced not idealistic, we discover in the same letter: "We have this treasure in earthenware vases, so that it may be seen that the extra-ordinary power comes from God, not from us" (2 Corinthians 4:7). Paul realizes that this extraordinary joy comes from God: he could not produce it by himself. It is a sign of transfiguration, not the fruit of a good character, not a natural or human gift. "We are troubled on every side but not crushed; we are disturbed but not desperate; per-secuted but not abandoned; struck but not killed, always bearing in our bodies the death of Jesus that the life of Jesus may also be manifested in our bodies" (2 Corinthians 4:8-10). It is not a state of tranquillity: it is a joy which takes into account all sorts of heaviness, all the difficult and unpleasant things which happen to him, all the misunder-standings and disagreements of daily life. It is the same with us. Paul was of a nervous disposition and therefore subject to depression and discouragement. As life goes on, he begins to realize that however discouraged he may some-times feel, there is always a stronger power dwelling within him.

Also, it is a joy which is shared, it is for his community, not a private possession; it is a joy in the things that are

76

happening around him, in the communities which he is guiding. "We are helping towards your joy" (2 Corinthians 1:24). And, writing to the Philippians he describes the community as "my joy and my crown" (Philippians 4:1). Let us not be deceived into thinking that it was an ideal or perfect community: rather, we know from the letter that Paul has to beg them almost on his knees not to engage in law suits, not to attack each other and cause divisions: "Do nothing out of a spirit of rivalry and vainglory" (Philippians 2:3). It means that there was rivalry and vainglory, that the community was by no means easy and caused him problems and worries. But he is able to think of it as his joy because he has been given a vision of faith which reaches beyond the purely pragmatic and the habitual, routine facts. It is a truly supernatural gift, the power of the Spirit which was always strong within him.

b) The second inner attitude, which arises from the first, is the *capacity for thanksgiving*. He exhorts his people to give joyful thanks to the Father (Colossians 1:12). It is typical of the Apostle to link joy with thanksgiving.

All his letters start with a prayer of thanksgiving except Galatians, which is a rebuke. Paul knows how to be thankful and his words are no empty formula but really express what he feels. Besides, the New Testament itself starts with a prayer of thanksgiving; in fact in all probability the oldest part of the New Testament, which pre-dates even the definitive form of the Gospels, is the first letter to the Thessalonians. So the first words of the New Testament are "Grace be to you and peace. I always give thanks to God for you all".

On the other hand, we never find in Paul any merely destructive criticism. There is reproof, never bitter resignation. His apostolic transfiguration, by God's gift, enables him always to see the good things first. To start every letter with thanksgiving means being able first of all to see the positive side of the community to which he is writing, even if there sometimes follow some extremely serious negative comments. At the start of the first letter to the Corinthians the community is praised as being full of wisdom and every kind of gift; then come the reproofs; but there is nothing incongruous about this. The eye of faith shows him that an ounce of faith in the hearts of his poor pagan converts is such an immense gift that it deserves endless praise to God.

The mature pastor has the ability to recognize the good around him, and to express his recognition with simplicity.

c) The third attitude is *praise*. In Paul we have those marvellous songs of praise which carry on the Jewish tradition of benedictions. He knows how to extend them so that they embrace the whole life of the community in Christ: For example, "Blessed be God, the Father of our Lord Jesus Christ, who has blessed us with all spiritual blessings in the heavens in Christ" (Ephesians 1:3). Paul's prayer, what we know of it from his letters, is primarily a prayer of praise. Thus he could value his darkest hours: "Blessed be God, the Father of our Lord Jesus Christ, the Father of mercy and God of all consolation, who himself comforts us" (2 Corinthians 1:3).

We could use his words to test our own attitude to praise: could we use them in the first person as an expression of our deepest selves or do we find it hard to say such things?

Praise is the characteristic attitude of the pastor who has been transfigured by the risen Christ and we should ask God to make it habitual with us. The devil is continually tempting us to fall back into worldly attitudes to life: sadness is the characteristic of a man whose horizons are limited. Sadness always seeks diversion and escape, anything which seems to make life happier and saves us from facing our sorrows.

The outward manifestations of Paul's transfiguration

a) The first external attitude is the *untiring ability to start again*, truly prodigious in Paul.

From the very first day of his conversion he preaches in Damascus and has to flee; he goes to Jerusalem and preaches and they make him leave; he stays at Tarsus until

Providence calls him back; when he is called back, forgetting past resentments, he starts off again. In his missionary journey, he has to begin afresh at nearly every stop; he preaches in Antioch in Pisidia, is chased away and goes to Iconium; at Iconium his life is threatened, they try to stone him and he goes to Lystra. At Lystra he is stoned. It is interesting to note Luke's impassive description of the scene: "Some Jews came from Antioch and Iconium and won over the crowd who stoned Paul and dragged him out of the city, thinking him dead. Then the disciples gathered round him and he got up and went into the city. The next day he left with Barnabas on the road to Derbe. Having preached the Gospel in that city and made a considerable number of disciples, they returned to Lystra, Iconium and Antioch" (Acts 14:19-21).

Most of his life is like that: he leaves Athens humiliated, mocked by the philosophers, but he goes to Corinth and starts again although he feels very much afraid.

This ability to start again is not human: after a few failed attempts a man is, humanly speaking, exhausted. We are not indefatigable and nor was he: it is a reflection of what he calls 'charity'. "Charity is never weary" (1 Corinthians 13:7). It is the love of God: "The love of God has been poured into our hearts by the Holy Spirit which has been given to us" (Romans 5:5). This love, poured out from on high, is a gift and that is why his disappointment is never definitive. "We are even proud of our sufferings because we know that suffering produces patience and patience experience and experience hope. And hope does not disappoint us because the love of God has been poured into our hearts by the Holy Spirit which has been given to us" (Romans 5:3-5).

If these words had been spoken by a new convert in his first enthusiasm, we might think that he was speaking without experience. Spoken by a missionary who has been through twenty years of trial they have a different ring and make us think deeply. No human power can acquire this attitude: it is the love of God shed forth in our hearts by the Spirit which is given to us.

Once again the transfiguration of Paul is the power of the risen Christ entering into his weakness and living in him.

b) The second exterior attitude is *liberty of spirit*. He seems to have reached a point where he no longer acts by constraint or in conformity to external patterns; he acts because of an inner strength. So he can assume bold attitudes which it would be rash to imitate. We see this liberty of spirit in the letter to the Galatians when he says that from a human standpoint it would have been more prudent to circumcise Titus in accordance with the requests of the Jewish Christians: "However, we did not agree to this for a moment so that the truth of the Gospel might be firmly upheld among you" (Galatians 2 : 5). Paul is not influenced by any judgment or current opinion: it is very difficult to go on in isolation in the face of a common opinion and a hostile culture. He does it with the utmost liberty, without self-pity, because his inner wealth is not to be compared with the weight of others' opinions. This strength of his allows him to a certain extent to oppose even Cephas. It is a borderline case of liberty: "(At Antioch) also the other Jews joined in Peter's pretence, so that even Barnabas was carried away by their hypocrisy" (Galatians 2 : 13). What he calls hypocrisy was evidently Barnabas' desire to mediate between the parties. Paul does not yield and it is his resistance which clarifies the situation.

This liberty is not arbitrary or presumptuous but springs from Paul's sense that as a servant of Christ he belongs to him absolutely and totally, like a slave. So Paul equates being a servant of Christ with being free from all other human opinions.

In this light, liberty becomes a most rigorous form of service: "Christ has liberated us so that we might be free; stand firm then and do not allow anyone to enslave you afresh. See, I Paul, tell you: If you have yourselves circumcised, Christ will be of no use to you. I declare once again to everyone who has himself circumcised that he is obliged to observe the whole Law. Christ cannot save you if you seek justification in the Law; you have fallen from grace.

For, through the Spirit, we expect to be justified by faith.
For in Christ Jesus it is not circumcision that counts but
faith, which works through love. You were running so well:
who got in your way so that you are no longer obedient to
the truth? This idea certainly did not come from the One
who is calling you! A little yeast leavens the whole of the
dough. I have confidence in you through the Lord that you
will not think otherwise; but the one who is upsetting you
has his judgment coming to him, whoever he is. As for me,
brothers, if I am still preaching circumcision, why am I
still being persecuted? Has the Cross then ceased to be a
stumbling-block? The people who are troubling you should
mutilate themselves! You, brothers, are called to liberty.
Only do not let this liberty become a pretext" — and we
know how often the word 'liberty' can be merely a pretext
— "to live according to nature, but serve one another
in love" (Galatians 5:1-13). This is one of the few passages
in which to 'serve' — in Greek to 'be the slave of' —
applies to one's fellowmen. The absoluteness of service to
Christ frees a man to the point where he is unafraid to
enslave himself to his brothers. So this liberty is a source
of the most humble service and is the root of that "in all
humility" which characterizes Paul's apostolate.

It is difficult to express these things in words without
minimizing and trivializing them: any attempt to do so
throws us back onto the inspired texts themselves — we
need to allow Paul's words to act upon us in all their original
force.

**Paul's transfiguration is the model for the transfiguration
of the pastor**

Let us now think about ways and means of acquiring
and maintaining this state of transfiguration.

Paul begins to be a pastor after Christ's heart after
fifteen years of labour and suffering. He does not do this
by his own efforts but by the gift of God.

The fundamental means of achieving transfiguration is
to realize that it is God, in his mercy, who brings it about.

The *primary means* of receiving the divine gift is contemplation, in the light of the Spirit, of the heart of Christ crucified. We could call this eucharistic contemplation: taking seriously the twofold table of the Word of God and the Eucharist, allowing ourselves to be nourished by the Word of God as a force which makes clear the historic and salvific meaning of the food which is the dead and risen Christ. This food becomes our nourishment and places us in the history of salvation while the Word of God communicates to us the reality and fullness and direction of that salvation.

For us, as for Paul, this contemplation is the way to transfiguration. The Apostle prayed ceaselessly and long, contemplating Christ, the dead and risen Lord.

— The gift of a heart transfigured by joy, praise, thankfulness, perseverance and liberty is gained by the intercession of Mary.

Mary, as mystery of God in the history of the Church and of salvation, is the one who sustains and feeds the light of faith in our hearts. Mature Christian experience is able to discern the place of the Virgin as model and intercessor, leading us towards a humble dependence on the Word of God which transfigures us, helping us to remain open at all times to the renewing power of the Spirit. Mary calls us to live in the midst of the Church at the same level of contemplation and prayerful listening as she does.

— The gift of pastoral transfiguration also comes through *sharing*, the ability to cling in the darkness to the one who can see the light. This is what our ecclesiastical and priestly communion means: to hold the hand of the one who sees the light — and to let him do the same to you as occasion offers.

This is where spiritual direction and penitential dialogue come in, both very important because they mean holding one another's hands, the practical way of opening our hearts and conserving those gifts of transfiguration which we admire so much in Paul.

— The gift of transfiguration requires evangelical *vigilance*. "Watch and pray so as not to fall into temptation"; "the spirit is willing but the flesh is weak"; "watch and stand firm in the faith". This repeated invitation is really a warning, expressing as it does the basic intuition that man is a creature of time who grows weary and is by nature incapable of perseverance.

Every Christian, every bishop and priest should know that no one is sure of final perseverance and that the greatest danger is to think that one has become so steadfast that no further precautions are necessary. The New Testament call to vigilance tells us that up to the hour of our death the devil will try to destroy our joy, faith and praise. We are constantly being attacked with regard to these fundamental attitudes.

We must be vigilant, knowing that there is no respite in this battle, and that we can quickly become weary, nervous and irritable again, or can dissipate ourselves in outward pleasures which weaken our faith. Paul returns often to the theme of vigilance and perseverance in prayer.

Let us ask for the prayers of Mary that we may watch with her, with Jesus and Paul, so that our apostolic transfiguration may be complete — and may our pastoral life be such that, despite the difficulties, sufferings and disappointments, we may be held firmly in the hands of God, deeply united to Christ.

Passio Pauli, passio Christi

The term 'passio Pauli', the passion of Paul, is commonly used to describe chapters 21 to 28 of the Acts of the Apostles, that is, the last part of the book: from his imprisonment in Jerusalem to his imprisonment in Rome.

I would like to extend the 'passion of Paul' to the succession of sufferings about which we learn partly from references in the letters and partly from tradition. It is strange that the Acts of the Apostles does not give the whole life of Paul but stops at a certain point and then introduces the chapters on his 'passion'. His apostolic activity takes up as many chapters as does the description of the imprisonment, trial and final imprisonment in Rome.

In the Gospels, too; the passion of Christ is given a very full treatment compared with the brevity of the preceding narrative of his life. The evangelist takes brief note of two or three years of Christ's public life, while he describes the passion almost hour by hour and minute by minute.

We can gather from this the importance which the evangelist and the early Church attach to the passion of Christ and the passion of Paul.

It is above all in the passion that the evangelist saw Christ as the Messiah who shows us the Father.

The same thing happens with Paul who bears witness to Christ not only in stirring or learned or deeply tender speeches, but also by being imprisoned, brought before tribunals, transferred from one prison to another, unsure of his fate, with his liberty severely curtailed, going in fear of death.

In this meditation let us ask for special grace to understand the mysterious sentence in the letter to the Philippians: "That I may know him by the power of his resurrection and by sharing his sufferings" (Philippians 3:10). Paul desires to know Jesus by entering into a mysterious, even physical communion with his sufferings.

You know, Father of mercy, how important it is for us to comprehend the mysterious communion with the sufferings of Christ. You know how difficult it is for us, how far removed from our way of thinking, how constantly denied in our everyday speech. That is why we humbly ask you, with Paul, to open the eyes of our hearts and minds so that we may know Christ and the power of his resurrection and, sharing Christ's sufferings, may offer our lives for the body of Christ.

Enlighten our minds, O Lord, that we may understand the words of Scripture, inflame our hearts so that we may realize that these words are not far removed from us but part of our own lives and the key to our own experience and to that of so many others in the world today.

We ask this, Father, with Mary, Mother of Sorrows, and with Paul, for the glory of Jesus, dead and risen for us, who lives and reigns in the Church and in the world through endless ages of ages. Amen.

Let us try to answer these questions:
— what is the passion of the Christian?
— how does Paul experience his passion?
— how should we experience ours?

Similarities and differences between 'passio Christi' and 'passio Pauli'

Let us look at some the stages of Christ's passion, comparing it with Paul's. We shall concentrate on three aspects:
— the arrest of Christ and the arrest of Paul;
— Christ and Paul before the tribunals;
— the physical and mental sufferings of Christ and Paul.

The arrest of Christ and the arrest of Paul

"While he was still speaking, there appeared a crowd of people; Judas, one of the Twelve, was at their head and he went up to Jesus to kiss him. Jesus said to him: Judas are you betraying the Son of Man with a kiss? Then those who were with him seeing what was going to happen, said: Lord, should we strike them with the sword?" (Luke 22:47-49).

Paul was in the Temple awaiting the days of Purification "when the Jews of the province of Asia, seeing him in the Temple, stirred up the whole crowd and laid hands on him shouting: Men of Israel, help! This is the man who goes about everywhere teaching against the people, the Law and this place; now he has even brought Greeks into the Temple and has profaned this holy place!" (Acts 21:27-29). The whole city is in an uproar. Paul is dragged out of the Temple, they lock the gates, they try to kill him. When the tribune arrives with a cohort, they arrest him and bind him with two chains. From that moment Paul is in prison for a very long time. What, then, have these two very different scenes in common?

In both cases the arrest is both treacherous and unjust: it is a surprise arrest with an ambush. They lay in wait for Jesus and for Paul; in each case, it is an ambush specially laid by enemies.

In both cases the arrest occurs at a moment when they are spending themselves for their own people. For Jesus it comes during a night of prayer, for Paul at the time of the offertory when, having brought gifts for his own people, he had even agreed to join in the rites of purification in the Temple. They are both taken prisoner at the very moment of apostolic dedication and service.

Christ and Paul before the tribunals

Jesus comes before several tribunals the Sanhedrin; Pilate's tribunal; he is interrogated and at first he responds to various accusations but after a certain point, he remains silent. Paul's trial is described more fully and is marked by a long series of speeches: the speech on the Temple steps in Acts 22, before the Sanhedrin in chapter 23, before Felix in chapter 24, before Festus in chapter 25 and King Agrippa in chapter 26. Paul makes a whole series of speeches in self-defence whereas Jesus only says a few words.

It is interesting to note the difference between the two situations: Paul is no slavish imitator of Jesus. He feels that he has the Spirit of God within him and, inspired by the Master's life, he responds to the situation on his own responsibility and behaves with firmness and dignity. He imitates Jesus' dignity, sense of justice and nobility of soul; but he acts differently, trying to confound his enemies by a full and spirited self-defence; and he succeeds in dividing the Sanhedrin by making his accusers argue among themselves.

Jesus affirms his adherence to his own mission in a few short and courageous words: "You said it, you say that I am a king; you will see the Son Man seated on the right hand of the power of God".

In both trials, we see personal interests, fears, clashes of individual or party ambition, behind an outward show of justice. Both Jesus and Paul are subjected to the uncertainties of human judgment and even if Paul could have had some hope of acquittal — in his letters he had always insisted on respect for authority — it is obvious that personal gain, greed and meanness prevail even in those who should have been administering justice.

The physical suffering of Christ and Paul

The sufferings of Jesus seem much greater because they are fully described in the accounts of the passion. In Paul's case we can only guess at the hardships of imprisonment: in fact he had already undergone considerable suffering in the floggings and stoning to which he had been subjected. He refers to them almost as something to be expected.

Paul lays more stress on moral sufferings, above all loneliness. This aspect is the one which most closely links our own passion to those of Christ and Paul.

Certainly the deepest moral sufferings undergone by Christ were due to his being totally abandoned by men. They all flee: only Peter follows him from a distance and then denies him. Jesus who was, after all, used to having someone to support him — and this is a habit one gets into — finds himself reduced to the most complete solitude. This solitude is increased by the mysterious abandonment by God, which is expressed in the cry: "My God, my God, why have you forsaken me?" A great deal has been written in an attempt to understand the meaning of this.

Perhaps the most dramatic and beautiful pages ever written on this subject are by Hans Urs von Balthasar in his *Paschal Mystery*: taking these words as his starting-point, he tries to interpret Good Friday from Jesus' point of view, with the darkness which enveloped his soul and the descent into hell. Balthasar works on the principle that we can interpret the passion of Jesus by looking at the passion of the saints: by understanding the darkness, desolation and dramatic experiences of abandonment in the lives of the great saints, we can grasp something of what Jesus went through first of all, on behalf of all and for the comfort and support of all of us.

What shall we say of Paul's moral sufferings? Paul's passion is a long process which lasts until the end of his life and consists in progressive abandonment by his disciples. He who is so full of vitality, comes out with statements that clearly show that he is weary and has suffered to the limits of his endurance; he says: "Try to come to me [these are the words of a man who really cannot cope anymore] because Demas, preferring this present world, has abandoned me and has gone to Thessalonica; Crescens has gone to Galatia, Titus to Dalmatia [as if to say: here I am on my own]. Only Luke is with us. Take Mark and bring him with you because he will be useful to me in the ministry". And he goes on: "Alexander the coppersmith has done me much harm. The Lord will repay him according to his deeds; you be careful of him too, because he has been a ruthless opponent of our preaching. No one came to be with me at my trial before the tribunal; they have all abandoned me. May it not be held against them" (2 Timothy 4:9-11, 14-16). That last sentence is the hardest of all.

This is a different Paul from the one we are used to: he is physically tired as well, worn out by imprisonment as is evident in the other 'pastoral' letters to Timothy and Titus. At this point we are not concerned to establish whether or not these letters are Pauline or if they record his actual words; we can take them as the Church has handed them down to us, as an expression of the figure of the Apostle as known and relayed to us by the early Church.

Certainly they give us a picture of Paul at a low ebb. He is no longer the enthusiast of Galatians and Romans with their great theological syntheses. He is a man who fights a lonely battle against daily odds, and even betrays a certain pessimism. He denounces the present state of affairs and foresees future ills; a dark and mournful tone has replaced his former hope, boldness and fervour.

This trial through which Paul went is a real trial, in which he realizes that he is no longer in complete command of himself, no longer able to be optimistic and enthusiastic; rather he has to reckon with fatigue and the accumulation of his worries and disappointments. God wants to show us, by Paul's experience, that man is purified by many means and this is a profound form of purification.

We can ask ourselves at this point if Paul also felt himself abandoned by God and suffered from interior darkness, desolation, the dark night of the soul. It is impossible to determine this from what Paul says of himself. However, he speaks several times of the dark forces of evil which seek to overshadow man's life, holding him in a merciless grip. So he is acquainted with these forces of darkness which continually threaten our innermost being.

If we go by what Balthasar says about Jesus, we may conclude that Paul, too, probably went through times when his faith was shrouded in darkness and he had to go on with a mere memory of the riches he possessed, no longer feeling aware of the presence of God.

The passion of the Christian

Some time ago, I was struck by a book which describes Thérèse of Lisieux's trial of faith. The latter part of the saint's life was extremely dark, and after the wonderful gifts she had received from God, she entered a state which is almost incomprehensible. She herself says that it is an unspeakable trial for the soul and she is almost afraid to talk of it. Then she writes: "It is as if I had been born in a country shrouded in thick fog, I have never seen nature smiling and transformed by the full splendour of sunlight; . . . all of a sudden the darkness which surrounds me becomes thicker and penetrates my soul and envelops it in such a way that I can no longer even imagine the sweet picture of my homeland; everything has disappeared! When I want to give my weary heart a rest from the darkness which surrounds it, by calling to mind the bright country to which I aspire, my torment is redoubled; it seems that the darkness, speaking with the voice of the unbeliever, mocks me: You dream of light, of a sweet and fragrant country, you dream of possessing eternally the Creator of all these marvels, you believe that one day you will emerge from the fog which surrounds you. Dream on! Find your happiness in death, which will give you, not what you hope for, but an even deeper night, the night of nothingness". And again: "When I sing of the joys of heaven and the eternal possession of God, I feel no joy at all, because I am singing merely of what *I want to believe*. It is true that sometimes a small ray of light shines down into my darkness; then my trial has a momentary respite but immediately afterwards the memory of this light, instead of cheering me, only serves to increase my darkness". "It is pure agony", she says on 30th September, the day of her death, "without any trace of consolation".

This is strong language. Perhaps even more forceful are these words, reported by a fellow-sister at the process of beatification: "If you knew the darkness I am in; I do not believe in eternal life, it seems to me that after this world there is nothing more. I have lost sight of everything; the only thing I have left is love".

She feels as if she no longer believes but she senses that love is still there: this is not a contradiction, it is the terrible purification of charity. These are experiences which are part of the Christian journey.

We can find similar confessions in other saints also. In his last illness, St Paul of the Cross comes out with remarks which really make one think. He confides to one of his brethren: "Today I felt the strongest urge to run out and disappear into the woods; I felt like throwing myself out of a window — suicidal temptations — and I am still strongly tempted to despair". And again: "A soul which has known the caresses of divine love and then finds itself for a while stripped of everything, apparently abandoned and no longer wanted by God, feeling that God no longer cares for him and is angry with him — such a soul has the impression that it can do nothing good. Ah, I cannot explain it as I would like to! Enough for you to know that it is almost like the torments of the damned, the very worst sort of punishment".

And then: "The feeling of having no more faith, hope or charity, of feeling as it were lost in the midst of a stormy sea without anyone in heaven or on earth to throw you a life-line. He has no light at all from God, is incapable of the least good thought, unable to discuss any point of the spiritual life, desolate like the mountains of Gilboa and cold as ice. Even in vocal prayer I can do no more than tell the beads of my rosary".

One of his brethren relates: "Coming into his room when he was ill, I heard him say three times in a voice which would have melted the hardest heart: I have been abandoned".

Certainly people's characters are an important factor here. The highly sensitive man will speak like this of himself in moments of fatigue, depression and illness. In any case it is true that God mysteriously permits his saints to undergo the trial of abandonment. It is a real situation and when it happens we should remember that it is the way of Christ on the cross, the way of Paul and many other saints.

When Paul wrote to Timothy, immediately after saying "Everyone has abandoned me", he affirmed: "But the Lord has been with me to strengthen me . . . the Lord will deliver me from all evil and will save me from eternal life; glory be to him throughout the ages" (2 Timothy 4: 17-18).

The power of the Spirit within him allowed him to overcome at a time when he could have been tempted to absolute despair. We cannot know, however, whether the last quarter of an hour of his life was clear and bright or shrouded in darkness. Man goes on his mysterious way towards the experience of death.

This is why we need to reflect on our own lives, on the sufferings through which others may pass and on the necessity of knowing how to give help. A sick man, especially if he is seriously ill, has difficulty in baring his soul: perhaps he will only do this to someone whom he trusts completely. Our task is to encourage such trust so that we can help people in the temptations against faith and hope which can assault the dying.

We are told that, towards the end of her life, Thérèse of the Child Jesus was seized by such distress and unutterable anguish that it frightened her sisters. They heard her say: "How the dying need prayer! If only you knew!"

This is how the lives of the saints can help us to a deeper understanding of the passion of Christ and the passion of Paul.

How Paul particularly shared in the passion of Christ

— From the letters in which Paul speaks of his sufferings we can see that first of all God gave him the ability to suffer in *a great spirit of faith* which enabled him to give his sufferings a clearly salvific value. ". . . the Saviour, our Lord Jesus Christ . . . on whose behalf I am herald, apostle and teacher. That is the cause of the evils I suffer" (2 Timothy 1:9-11).

If I suffer, I suffer for Christ and "I am not ashamed of it: for I know in whom I have believed and I am convinced that he is able to keep what has been entrusted to me until that day" (2 Timothy 1:12).

— For the one who suffers, the spirit of faith is imbued with a *sense of the Church*. "Remember that Jesus Christ, of the stock of David, rose from the dead according to my Gospel, for which I suffer to the point of being in chains like a criminal; but the word of God is not chained! Therefore I endure everything for the elect, so that they may also attain the salvation and eternal glory which is in Christ Jesus" (2 Timothy 2:8-10). I suffer, but it is for others, for the whole Church, for the work of Christ. "I am happy to suffer for your sake and I complete in my body what is lacking to the sufferings of Christ for the sake of his body, the Church. I have become a minister of the Church in order to carry out the mission to you with which God entrusted me: to fulfil the word of God" (Colossians 1:24-25). Paul has a very deep sense of mission, which is the mainspring of everything he does for the Church, and he does not abandon this even at such difficult times; rather it gives him the grace to consider his sufferings as the completion of the service which he desires to render to the very end.

Questions for us

We can end by asking ourselves what is our own attitude.

Above all we need to realize that we are extremely frail and liable to be tempted perhaps even in little things, and yet we must go through these difficult times. The sense of our frailty is important because otherwise we run the risk of speaking of these things in a facile way and when we find ourselves experiencing them our reaction is quite the opposite and we soon change our tune! The consciousness of our own frailty enables us to make a more intelligent connection between what we read and what we experience in fact.

For this, it is necessary to exercise the vigilance already mentioned, of which Paul often reminds us: "And when people say: all is now peaceful and secure, then ruin will suddenly strike you, like the labour pains of a woman; and no one will be able to escape. But you, brothers, are not in darkness so that that day should surprise you like a thief: you are all children of light and sons of the day; we do not belong to darkness and night. So let us not sleep as others do, but let us keep sober and watchful" (1 Thessalonians 5:3-6).

"Put on the armour of faith and love, with the hope of salvation as your helmet" (1 Thessalonians 5:8). "Put on the armour of God so that you may be able to resist the devil's wiles. For we fight, not against flesh and blood but against the principalities and powers, the rulers of the realm of darkness, and the evil spirits which live in the heavens. So take up the armour of God so that you will be able to resist in the time of evil and stand firm after having overcome all your trials" (Ephesians 6: 11-13).

Christian life is no short-lived trial because we are continually confronted and repeatedly assaulted by an implacable foe. When we look at daily reality and the simple things which make up our day, this sort of language seems excessive; but if we look more deeply into our own lives and those of others, if we think about the bitter trials people undergo, the problems which lead them to anguish and despair, then we can see much more clearly that the enemy of man is at work. The devil uses the simplest, most hidden and underhand methods to undermine our faith and hope, suggesting that we should resign ourselves to life's ills rather than see them in the light of God's saving action. He is continually seeking to extinguish the light of faith which allows us to see everything as a means of progress towards the God who is continually coming to us even in the midst of pain.

The New Testament exhorts us to vigilance and warfare because it is well aware of the human condition and knows that all of us must undergo trials; when we think they are over, we find that they are closer than ever before.

As we meditate on the passion of Christ and the passion of Paul, let us ask the Lord to help us to walk in God's ways, to remain upright, bravely facing our difficulties; may we also be able to help others, many others, not to be defeated by their trials.

God is mercy

Let us conclude these meditations by looking at the last part of Paul's speech at Miletus: this is his final pastoral exhortation before the start of his passion.

According to Acts, it was at Miletus that Paul made his last public speech. For this reason it has a special significance, being a résumé of his own desires as well as showing how the early Church thought of Paul.

As we look at Paul's last words, let us ask that we may understand them in the spirit in which he spoke them; may we perceive the truth which they have for us today as the living and powerful Word of God.

We thank you, Lord, that these words of Paul spoken two thousand years ago, have life and power for us today.

We are aware of our powerlessness and inability to understand and let these words live within us. These words are stronger and more potent than our weakness, stronger than our frailty, able to overcome all our resistance.

So we ask you to enlighten us by your Word; may we take it to heart, opening ourselves to its message that it may have free course in our lives, working in us according to the riches of its power.

Mother of Jesus, who gave yourself without reserve, asking that the word which had been spoken to you might be fulfilled, give us the spirit of availability so that we may discover our own truth. Grant that we may help all men to discover God's truth in their lives, and may the world and our society also come into this fullness of truth, this world which we humbly desire to serve.

We ask this, Father, through Christ Jesus your incarnate Word, by his death and resurrection and by the

Holy Spirit who continually renews the power of this Word within us, now and forever. Amen.

"And now I entrust you to the Lord and to the Word of his grace which has the power to build you up and give you an inheritance among all the saints" (Acts 20:32).

This, the solemn conclusion of the speech, is the passage on which we will meditate. As we shall see, it also has the value of a liturgical prayer and a blessing. Let us note, however, that after this passage there is an addition, as if Paul wished to insist on a subject which he has at heart: "I have not coveted anyone's silver or gold or clothing. You know that I have supported myself and my companions by the work of my own hands. In every way I have shown you that by working in such a way you ought to support the weak, remembering the words of the Lord Jesus who said: It is a happier thing to give than to receive" (Acts 20:33-35).

Chronologically speaking, then, this is the marvellous final sentence which sums up Paul's experience: "It is a happier thing to give than to receive".

However, let us stop at the 'official' ending which provides an equally significant conclusion to his pastoral life.

What place, in fact, does this final passage hold in the structure of the Miletus speech?

Paul has spoken to the elders; now he has to leave them and he is concerned with their future activities. In their turn, the elders are wondering how they are going to carry on their communal task.

So this is Paul's answer, his last advice and his final legacy to the community.

It may be helpful to find a parallel here in the life of Jesus. According to John's Gospel, Jesus' last words, summing up what he has done, are: "I have made your name known to them and I shall continue to do so, so that your love for me may be in them and that I may be in them" (John 17:26). According to Luke's Gospel, Jesus' last words are a call to vigilance: "Watch and pray continually so that you may escape all these coming events and stand before the Son of Man" (Luke 21:36). This same call is echoed just before the end of the speech at Miletus.

The ending to Mark's Gospel is similar, while Matthew ends with the judgment on works of mercy (the parable of the sheep and the goats).

Each evangelist ends his account of Jesus' public preaching with the thing which is particularly significant to him.

Thus the Acts conclude their account of the Apostle's public life with a sentence which is significant of all that Paul is, all that he preaches, believes and practises.

Let us now examine this sentence more closely.

Paul's last words

— "*And now*": the Greek term 'kai ta nun' is fairly rare and unusual in the New Testament.

It means: "So, in this present situation". The situation in which you are to be parted from me, facing an uncertain future, afraid of what might happen to you.

This is a solemn formula of conclusion which we find, for example, at the end of the apostles' prayer during the first persecution. Having said: "Lord, you who made heaven and earth, the sea . . . you said by the mouth of David:

'Why are the heathen in an uproar
And why do the people hatch useless plots?
The kings of the earth rose up
And the princes were gathered together
Against the Lord and against his Anointed'.

Truly they were gathered together in this city against your holy servant Jesus" (Acts 4:24-27). The prayer ends: "And now [kai ta nun], Lord, see how they threaten us and grant your servants boldness to preach your Word" (Acts 4:29).

In the same way, Paul's expression presupposes the whole situation which he has previously outlined: his ministry in the community, their mutual affection, the future dangers and above all the fear of what is to befall them. That is why he concludes with: "And now . . .".

97

— *"I entrust you to the Lord"*. This phrase astonishes us. We would have expected him to exhort them to be faithful and united, to write to him, to hold meetings, to give him the news, to keep up their Bible reading.

Instead, Paul entrusts them to God, thus stressing that the future and their perseverance are in the hands of God: it is he who receives and sustains us. This is a conclusion fairly commonly employed by the early Church in similar situations. At the end of the first missionary journey, on the way back, Barnabas and Paul put fresh heart into the disciples, exhorting them to be steadfast in the faith; they appointed elders for every church and having prayed and fasted, "they entrusted them to the Lord in whom they had believed" (Acts 14:23). And a little later: "They set sail for Antioch from where they had originally set out, entrusted to the grace of God" (Acts 14:26).

So it is the custom of the community to entrust themselves quite explicitly to the Lord and his grace. Commendation to God with prayer and fasting is a solemn liturgical form. We can imagine that it was performed with outstretched hands and the words: "See, we commit you to the power of God".

The very verb to 'commit' or 'entrust' has a very long history.

In the New Testament it refers to a concrete reality, the commitment of a precious treasure to someone whom one trusts: I have a treasure, I have to go away and I leave it in the hands of a trusted person. It is true that the use of the term which we find in the New Testament is profane, but it explains the mentality behind it and finds its highest expression in Jesus' words on the cross: "Father, into your hands I commend my spirit" (Luke 23:46). It is the act of supreme trust: Jesus commits his whole being, his life and death into the hands of God, knowing that he will guard it and give it to him again. He stakes everything on his faith in the divine power.

The psalm quoted by Jesus: "Into your hands I commend my spirit, you will redeem me; O set me free, Lord God in whom I trust" (Psalm 31:6) is the expression of a man who, having thought it all over, knows that the only thing that counts is to commit oneself into the hands of God.

We can say that man, having done his utmost on the level of 'works', returns to his fundamental level of dependence on God and, in so doing, realizes that being human involves just such a dependence.

Paul, while he is concerned about his much-loved community, is sure that God will carry on the work, sustaining, enlightening and guiding it. Paul's words of trust mark the height of pastoral affection and also of detachment. Paul loves this community very much; he takes his leave and embraces them with tears and prayers on the shore near the ship — but he knows that it belongs to God and that God is infinitely more powerful.

— *"and the Word of his grace"*. This is an unusual expression and we must try to clarify it.

Luke's Gospel gives it as a first definition of Jesus' words. In the synagogue at Nazareth, in fact, when the people hear him "they all saw him and were amazed at the gracious words which came from his lips" (Luke 4:22).

So we can say that the word of grace is a synonym for the Gospel, the manifestation of divine initiative, bringing the free gift of salvation. This is the meaning of the term 'of grace' — 'charitos'. It comes from 'charis' (grace), and the word 'chara' (joy) also comes from the same root, as does 'gratis', used by Paul to signify God's action in forgiving the sinner through no merit of his own.

Mary will be saluted by the Angel as 'kecharitomene' (Luke 1:28), that is, 'exceedingly graced', the object of God's full and unlimited favour.

It is a typical New Testament word: it occurs 155 times and about 100 times in Paul. Paul uses the term 'grace' along with others: saving justice, faith, Gospel, hope, Spirit, all realities which he mentions when he wishes to speak of the positive divine economy in regard to men. Against these he sets: the Law, sin, boastfulness, the flesh, which all signify the negative and restrictive economy in which man tends to enclose himself through pride, self-sufficiency, weakness and malice.

For Paul, the whole Christian apostolate consists in proclaiming the grace of God who is rich in mercy. "As we are his fellow-workers, we exhort you not to receive God's grace in vain [that is the definition of the evangelist!]. For God says: At a favourable time I heard you and in the day of salvation I came to your aid. This is the favourable time, now is the day of salvation" (2 Corinthians 6:1-2). That is a summary of the apostolic preaching. The renewing, transforming aspect of God's revelation, expressed by the word 'grace' which suggests an absolutely free and spontaneous divine action, beyond any merit or resistance of ours. God is greater than our hearts.

The definition in the second letter to the Corinthians is followed by the description of an apostle which shows the characteristic features of this grace: "In all things we act as the ministers of God, steadfast in time of trouble, need and distress; in floggings, imprisonment and riots, in toil and vigil and fast; by purity, wisdom and patience, by kindness and a spirit of holiness, by sincere love; by truthful speech, by the power of God; by the armour of righteousness on our right hand and on our left; in honour and disgrace, in good or bad repute. We are taken for imposters and yet we are genuine, we are unknown and yet well known; we seem to be dying and yet we are still alive; punished but not put to death; afflicted but always joyful; poor but enriching many; folk who have nothing and yet possess everything" (2 Corinthians 6:4-10).

The Apostle, preaching about grace, lives in such a way that worldly attitudes — depression, humiliation, fear, self-concern — give way to serenity, joy, steadfastness, the ability to enrich others: this is what it means to live the Gospel.

It is significant that, having given vent to this lengthy description of his own experience, Paul ends by saying: "We have spoken frankly and opened our hearts completely to you" (2 Corinthians 6:11). That is, he has revealed his whole inner being: the mystery of being the Apostle of grace means to experience this paradox: the circumstances which should have crushed him, in fact lead him to the humble avowal that God's prevenient action is at work in his life reversing the very situations which appeared, humanly speaking, to overwhelm him.

When the Apostle says: "I entrust you to the Word of grace", he is reminding his hearers that God manifests himself in Jesus the Word. Paul will no longer be with the community, he will no longer speak to them but the Word of God is theirs forever and the power of this Word can renew them with that free, prevenient action which makes up for every human weakness.

In the book of Acts there is constant reference to the Word as a person who acts and has power. In his Gospel, Luke writes that "the boy (Jesus) grew" (Luke 2:40). The Word is seen as Jesus himself, growing in the midst of the community; this Word lives and works and, through the Spirit, remains in the Church.

— "Which has power to edify". Several basic New Testament texts come to mind, above all the letter to the Romans which explicitly proclaims the power of God through the Gospel. It is also a farewell letter and we can read it as a liturgical expansion of Paul's final blessing of the community at Miletus: "To him who has power to confirm you according to my Gospel and the message of Jesus Christ, according to the mystery of the relevation hidden for centuries but now revealed and announced through the prophets, by the eternal ordinance of God, that all men might be obedient to the faith of the only-wise God, through Jesus Christ be glory forever. Amen" (Romans 16:25-27). Commitment to the divine power becomes a prayer, the doxology being an indication of the solemnity with which the Apostle pronounces it.

The Word has power to edify or build up all the activities of the community. The community is a body which grows with all its joints well fitted together, according to an inner hierarchy and order, having a wealth of different charisms. It is a body in the making and the Word of God is the power which builds it up. Both the contents and the message of this Word help to construct the building.

And Paul sees the future of the community which, remaining faithful to the primacy of the Word, will be built up with all the riches of various charisms, gifts, services and ministries.

— *"And give you an inheritance among all the saints"*. The Word of God also works towards the growth of the community, calling many others to share and enjoy this precious heritage.

Conclusion

So Paul leaves us, bearing witness to his total apostolic dedication and his profound detachment, which is a sign of his fidelity to the original intuition: it is God who saves, and it is to Jesus, who appeared to him on the road to Damascus, that he owes everything. If Jesus appeared to him in power while he was still a sinner, then this is valid also for the community and every single human being. Community is created, not because Paul has done something, but because Jesus mainfests himself in power and will continue to manifest himself in the heart of each member.

Long ago, Moses had heard this Word on the mountain: "I will make all my glory pass before your eyes and I will proclaim my Name of Lord before you. I will give grace to whom I please and I will have mercy on whom I please" (Exodus 33: 18-19).

In New Testament language, this means that God is the source of all mercy. It is not our efforts and application: when we have done all we can, the factor which will tip the balance is still the mercy of God.

It is he who saves us, he who loves us.

So now Paul bids us farewell for a while, having shared his testimony with us and helped us to enter into some of his rich experience.